CAREERS IN FILM AND TELEVISION

33,34,35

SO FI3.

SO YOU WANT
TO BE A FILM
OR TV EDITOR?

Amy Dunkleberger

Enslow Publishers, Inc.
40 Industrial Road
Box 398
Berkeley Heights, NJ 07922
USA

http://www.enslow.com

Library of Congress Cataloging-in-Publication Data

Dunkleberger, Amy.
   So you want to be a film or TV editor? / Amy Dunkleberger.
      p. cm. — (Careers in film and television)
   Includes bibliographical references and index.
   Summary: "Explains the history and fundamentals of film/sound editing, discusses the role of
   editors in the filmmaking process, analyzes scenes from Psycho and Apocalypse Now, and
   provides education and career advice from industry experts."—Provided by publisher.
   ISBN-13: 978-0-7660-2739-8
   ISBN-10: 0-7660-2739-2
   1. Motion pictures—Editing—Vocational guidance—Juvenile literature. 2. Television—
   Production and direction—Vocational guidance—Juvenile literature. 3. Sound—Recording
   and reproducing—Vocational guidance—Juvenile literature. I. Title.
   TR899.D86 2007
   791.4301—dc22

                               2006039767

Printed in the United States of America

10 9 8 7 6 5 4 3 2 1

To Our Readers:
We have done our best to make sure all Internet addresses in this book were active and
appropriate when we went to press. However, the author and the publisher have no control over
and assume no liability for the material available on those Internet sites or on other Web sites
they may link to. Any comments or suggestions can be sent by e-mail to
comments@enslow.com or to the address on the back cover.

Illustration Credits: AP/ Wide World Photos, p. 63; Jupiterimages Corporation,
pp. 4, 103; all other images courtesy of The Everett Collection, Inc.

Cover Illustration: Jupiterimages Corporation.

CONTENTS

INTRODUCTION

Just as screenwriting is the key component in the preproduction phase of filmmaking, and directing, the key during production, film editing is the key element of postproduction. From the first-cut assembly to the final tweaking of the music mix, editing is a varied and complex process. As veteran film editor Ralph Rosenblum (*Fail Safe, Annie Hall*) observed in his book *When the Shooting Stops . . . the Cutting Begins:*

> A feature-length film generates anywhere from twenty to forty hours of raw footage. When the shooting stops, that unrefined film becomes the movie's raw material, just as the script had been the raw material before. It must now be selected, tightened, paced, embellished, arranged, and in some scenes given artificial respiration, until the author's and the director's vision becomes completely translated from the language of the script to the idiom of the movies.[1]

1

IN THE BEGINNING THERE WAS THE CUT

Imagine the following movie opening: A young woman strolls down a school hallway, stopping in front of a locker. As her hand reaches casually for the combination lock, the film cuts to a shot of a young man looking in her direction from across the corridor. That shot is followed by a close-up of the lock dial being turned by the girl and then by a shot of the boy, biting his lips, his brow creased. In a final close-up, the lock drops open.

How are viewers likely to react to this series of shots? They will probably assume the boy knows something about the locker that the girl is unaware of, and that danger lurks behind its door. Is the boy going to warn her? Viewers will be holding their breaths to find out.

What if the scene were replayed without the close-ups of the lock? In their place are shots of a policeman approaching the girl from behind. The boy now appears to be reacting nervously to the policeman, not the lock. Although the girl's actions are exactly the same, viewers will no longer be worrying about what is inside her locker. Instead they will focus on the policeman and wonder about his relationship to the teenagers. By changing one or two shots, the story has changed dramatically.

Editors have many choices in how they put together a scene. How do they whittle down hours and hours of raw footage to one or two hours of movie magic? How do editors pick which shots to include, which shots to linger on, or which shots to shorten?

The editorial process is a mixture of creative instinct and rules based on common sense. "In the end," notes editor and film scholar Walter Murch (*Apocalypse Now*, *Jarhead*), "the editor of a film must try to take advantage of all the material that is given to him, and reveal it in a way that feels like a natural but exciting unfolding of the ideas of the film. It's really a question of orchestration: organizing the images and sounds in a way that is interesting . . . and understandable when it needs to be understandable."[1]

Editor-turned-director Edward Dmytryk declared about the role of the editor: "The truth, then, is that in spite of the time, talent, and effort spent in writing, preparing, and shooting a film, it has no shape or substance until the hundreds, even thousands, of bits and pieces which go to make it are assembled."[2]

EDWIN S. PORTER, THE EDITOR IS BORN

Filmmaker and historian Ernest Lindgren once claimed that the "development of film technique has been primarily the development of editing." Certainly the history of film art is all but inseparable from the history of film editing.

In the mid-1890s, the very first "big screen" movies were produced in France by the Lumiere brothers (Auguste and Louis). The Lumieres set up

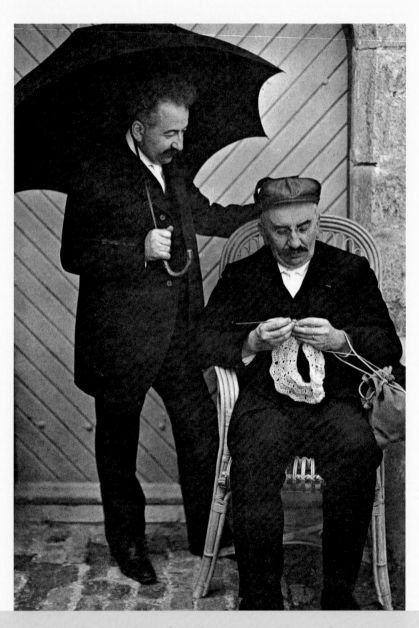

The Lumiere brothers, Auguste and Louis

their camera around Paris and filmed the world around them. Despite the movies' simplicity, audiences were dazzled, and even frightened, to see everyday events—a train entering a station, workers leaving a factory—projected as continuous pieces of action.

A few years later, in America, inventor and projectionist Edwin S. Porter teamed up with actor and scenic designer George S. Fleming to produce a series of short narrative films. Movies like *Kansas Saloon Smashers* and *Why Mr. Nation Wants a Divorce* ran less than a minute and consisted of one or two shots. Although many of them told little stories, the action was performed in front of a fixed camera, like a stage play. More significantly, the stories played out in real time. The running time of the film was the same as the running time of the action.

With *The Execution of Czologosz* (1901), a ninety-second re-creation of the execution of President William McKinley's assassin, however, Porter began to expand the world of cinematic storytelling. Included in the film were shots of both the outside and inside of the prison. The exterior shots established the film's setting, while the interior shots showed a series of separate but connected actions: the prisoner being led from his cell to the execution chamber, the electric chair being readied by prison employees, and finally Czologosz's electrocution.

Director Edwin Porter and cameraman Henry Cronjager work on a scene from Country Girls' Seminary Life and Experiences *at Edison Studios in the Bronx, New York, in 1908.*

Though simple and obvious by today's standards, Porter's design for the film was radical (so much so that his boss, inventor Thomas Edison, complained). Instead of focusing solely on the electrocution, Porter took time to set up the scene for the viewer. He included more shots than was normal for the time and cut them together in a way that was both logical and dynamic.

In the 1902 documentary short *Life of the American Fireman*, Porter began experimenting with overlapping action. At the beginning of the film, firemen are seen waking to an alarm, sliding down the fire pole, and racing to their truck. Instead of starting each shot with a new action, Porter repeated part of the action from the preceding shot. In shots three and four, for example, the firemen are seen sliding down the pole twice. This "stutter" effect appears awkward today but was a necessary step in the evolution of editing.

Porter's innovations gradually changed the way all films were conceived and made. According to Ralph Rosenblum, "When it came into being in 1902, film editing transformed motion pictures from a recording medium into an art form."[3]

In 1903, Porter took his editing techniques to the next level. *The Great Train Robbery* revolutionized movies by introducing parallel action and cross-cutting to the film narrative. Parallel action allowed the audience to follow two separate, simultaneous story lines at once—the train robbery in one location and the posse formation in another. Porter accomplished parallel action through cross-cutting, an editing technique in which shots from one setting are put next to shots from another setting. Through cross-cutting, which is often used for chase sequences,

CROSS-CUTTING—The alternating of shots from two sequences, usually in different locations, to suggest the action is going on at the same time.

Porter was able to build dramatic tension by condensing time and space.

D. W. GRIFFITH AND THE LANGUAGE OF FILM

The next wave of movie editing innovation began in 1908 with the emergence of filmmaker D. W. Griffith (1875–1948). Most cinema scholars consider Griffith the most important American figure in the development of film as an art form, and he has been called by many "the father of film language." The language Griffith devised was, for all intents and purposes, the language of editing.

Beginning with the short *The Adventures of Dollie*, Griffith made over four hundred silent films between 1908 and 1913. During those five years, Griffith expanded on editing techniques introduced by Porter. As a director, Griffith moved his camera closer to the action and increased the number of shots for each scene. In the editing room, he then mixed long shots, medium shots, and close-ups in such a way as to draw audiences deeper into the world of the film. The "Griffith formula," as it is sometimes called, became an editing standard still in use today.

With his controversial feature-length Civil War story *The Birth of a Nation* (1915), Griffith added a significant wrinkle to Porter's parallel action device. In addition to connecting two sets of simultaneous actions, as Porter did in *The Great Train Robbery*,

Griffith connected entire story lines through thematic editing. Shots of light- and dark-gray kittens playing in one setting were cut next to shots of Confederate and Union soldiers dressed in similarly colored uniforms.

Griffith used this type of parallel thematic editing in a more obvious way in his 1916 film *Intolerance*. In that four-hour epic, Griffith intertwined four different stories, set in four different time periods, to dramatize the broader story of man's inhumanity to man. Serving as a bridge, or transition, between the time periods was a single shot of a woman (Lillian Gish) rocking a baby in a cradle.

SERGEI EISENSTEIN AND THEMATIC EDITING

After Griffith introduced moviegoers to the idea of thematic editing, Russian filmmaker Sergei Eisenstein turned the device into a cinematic philosophy. In the 1920s, Eisenstein declared that editing, or montage as it was called, was the foundation of all moviemaking. A theoretician as well as a filmmaker, Eisenstein saw montage not just as a way to increase tension and excitement, but as a vital storytelling tool in its own right.

Rather than starting with a master long shot and cutting to increasingly closer shots, D. W. Griffith style, Eisenstein juxtaposed, or put together, shots of different subjects, often close-ups, to create a whole new meaning. Einsenstein believed that when one shot is put together with another, with each shot having its own dramatic meaning, a third, separate meaning, or idea, results.

In his 1925 silent classic *The Battleship Potemkin*, Eisenstein used his editorial techniques to dramatize the real-life story of social rebellion and unrest in the Russian town of Odessa. More than just depicting the uprising through action, Eisenstein juxtaposed shots that suggested symbolically the *idea* of rebellion.

The most famous sequence in *Battleship Potemkin* is known as the Odessa Steps sequence. Using 158 separate shots, some lasting only a quarter of a second, the sequence depicted the surprise massacre of Odessa citizens by rifle-toting Russian soldiers. In his introduction to the script of the film, Eisenstein noted that he designed the six-minute sequence to maximize the "mounting emotional intensity" of the attack. He then described how he achieved that emotional intensity through editing:

> First, there are *close-ups* of human figures rushing chaotically. Then, *long-shots* of the same scene. The *chaotic movement* is next superseded by shots showing the feet of soldiers as they march *rhythmically* down the steps. Tempo increases. Rhythm accelerates. And then, as the *downward* movement reaches its culmination, the movement is suddenly reversed: instead of the headlong rush of the *crowd* down the steps we

see the *solitary* figure of a mother carrying her dead son, *slowly* and *solemnly going up* the steps.[4]

Although Eisenstein's editing techniques may seem heavy-handed by today's standards, they nevertheless revolutionized the way filmmakers approached editing. More contemporary directors like Francis Ford Coppola have used thematic editing to great effect. For example, at the end of Coppola's *The Godfather* (1972), shots of Michael Corleone participating in his godchild's christening ceremony are intercut with shots of the brutal slayings of his gangster rivals. By cross-cutting between the two seemingly unrelated activities, the editing suggests the duality, and hypocrisy, of Michael's new life as a mafia don.

Likewise, footage at the end of *Apocalypse Now* (1979) showing the ritualistic slaying of a water buffalo in a Cambodian village is intercut with footage of a political assassination in the same village. Coppola intermingled images of the two attacks to comment symbolically on the primitive nature of the government-sanctioned assassination.

SLAVKO VORKAPICH, THE MONTAGE KING

In the early 1930s, Yugoslavia-born editor and theoretician Slavko Vorkapich developed what is now called a montage sequence. Like Eisenstein,

Vorkapich was also a film theoretician. In contrast to Eisenstein, however, Vorkapich believed strongly in the notion of visual linkage, that shots should be selected and joined because of what they already have in common. Vorkapich rejected Eisenstein's idea that editors should create meaning by juxtaposing images artificially.

At its most ordinary, a montage sequence contains many brief shots that, when strung together, convey the passage of time. Filmmakers use montages to dramatize actions that are necessary to the plot, but would slow the film's pace if depicted in full.

Montages often contain no dialogue, and many are edited to music. A classic "Vorkapich" montage might show the passage of time through shots of calendar pages falling away or a landscape changing from spring to winter. In the 1969 western *Butch Cassidy and the Sundance Kid*, the budding romance between Butch Cassidy (Paul Newman) and Etta (Katharine Ross) is depicted in a series of shots underscored by the pop song "Raindrops Keep Falling on My Head." The 2005 film *Walk the Line* included a montage, set to Johnny Cash's music, that summarized the singer's rise to recording fame and his growing attachment to fellow singer June Carter.

MUSIC VIDEOS AND
THE MTV FACTOR

The most recent notable artistic development in editing occurred in the 1980s with the arrival of music videos and MTV. In addition to changing the way television commercials were made, music videos gradually insinuated themselves into longer dramatic formats.

The first real move toward the modern music video occurred in 1964 with the Beatles' film *A Hard Day's Night*, directed by Richard Lester. In addition to its unusual visual elements, the movie boasted fresh, stylized editing. Lester and his editor, John Jympson, used fast-paced, jumpy cutting to underline the chaos of the rock life and the carefree energy of the Beatles' music.

In the late 1960s, similar techniques were used in the pop rock television show *The Monkees*. Between 1979 and 1981 Monkees member Michael Nesmith made what are considered to be the prototypes for the modern music video. Some were broadcast on the NBC show *Saturday Night Live*, while others were released on a "video record" called *Elephant Parts*.

Music videos took off in 1981 with the arrival of the twenty-four-hour television network MTV. The first music video broadcast on MTV was, appropriately, "Video Killed the Radio Star" by The Buggles. Over the next few years, the basic music video format evolved and blossomed.

Michael Jackson's "Thriller" video (above) was one of the most influential videos of the early MTV era.

Because music videos rarely contain dialogue, videomakers rely heavily on the visuals to convey their meaning. Many music videos blend performance or concert footage with storytelling. Others integrate the musical performance into the story. The story may have little to do with the lyrics of the song. The challenge of video editing then is to integrate the various elements while promoting and supporting the music.

A typical music video combines Eisenstein's thematic montage with D. W. Griffith's classic narrative editing. The tempo of the cuts is often fast, dictated in part by the tempo of the music. Jump cuts—cuts that show jumps in time and place—are common, as are cuts that connect seemingly unrelated subjects. Extreme close-ups edited against long shots also occur regularly in music videos.

The overall impact of music videos on movies and television was significant. The stars of the 1980s television series *Miami Vice* became known as "the MTV cops" because the show featured action set to popular music, edited with quick takes in the style of music videos. When *Flashdance* was released in 1983, some critics accused director Adrian Lyne of making a ninety-minute music video, but audiences loved the fresh approach. With their polished, nonrealistic blending

> **JUMP CUT**—Two similar shots cut together with a jump in continuity, camera position, or time.

of music and image, more recent movies like Oliver Stone's *Natural Born Killers* (1994) and Baz Luhrmann's *Moulin Rouge* (2003) owe much to music videos as well.

Today more and more television shows include popular music, sometimes played underneath stylized editing, as part of their standard format. Movie trailers are often cut together music video style—presenting a collage of images that are meant to appeal to the senses. To make the connection complete, many movies now promote themselves through music videos that weave bits of action from the movie into the visuals for the song.

EDITING FUNDAMENTALS

As already suggested, film editing operates on a variety of levels.

OVERALL STRUCTURE

The first and broadest level of editing exists in the film's overall structure. Screenwriters have first crack at the film's structure, the order and manner in which scenes are presented, and the story's spine, its dramatic arc. The script also includes such structural devices as flashbacks, voice-over narration, and parallel action.

Inevitably, however, some structural issues wind up in the hands of editors. Weaknesses in story organization may not become apparent until the film has been shot and scenes spliced together. The scene that seemed indispensable on the page may feel redundant or pointless up on the screen. Occasionally a movie's structure may be affected by an actor's performance. A poor performance may require that certain scenes are reduced or even eliminated, or an editor might decide that an end scene works better at the beginning.

SCENE STRUCTURE

At the next level, editors look at the structure of individual scenes. Like the director, the editor considers the dramatic objective of each scene. What do the characters want? What are their goals? What are they feeling at the start of the scene and where do they end up? The editor will assess footage based on these questions and either confirm the director's approach or offer alternatives.

Although many directors create preproduction storyboards detailing each scene's structure, some directors design scenes as they shoot or wait until they are in the editing room to make final decisions about their structure. It is not unusual for editors to suggest changes in shot selection or order, or to request that additional footage be shot.

How shots are assembled in the editing room is dependent in part on the scene's point of view. Subjective, or first-person, point of view usually requires an abundance of close shots, while objective, third-person point of view is accomplished through medium and long shots. Generally, questions about point of view are answered in the screenplay and through the director's shot selection, but the editor may end up altering a scene's narrative approach based on how the shots actually play on-screen.

The editor may also choose when and how to transition from one scene to the next. Just as it is in screenwriting, figuring out where to start and end a scene is one of the editor's trickiest tasks. Scene transitions, which may also involve a significant shift in time, have to be clear but economic.

Sometimes for effect, scenes that are related but not parallel, or simultaneous, are overlapped during editing. In an episode of *CSI: Crime Scene Investigation*, for example, a scene showing the investigators discussing the evidence in a murder case is intercut with shots of the guilty suspect being led away in handcuffs. The arrest actually takes place sometime after the discussion, but by interweaving the two scenes, the cause and effect between the investigators' work and the arrest is made clearer and stronger.

TRANSITIONAL EFFECTS

For extra emphasis, editors sometimes use simple effects—fade-ins, fade-outs, and dissolves—when transitioning between scenes. A fade-in is the slow brightening of the image from blackness to normal lighting. A fade-out reverses the process, from light to dark. Editors use fade-ins and fade-outs at the beginning and end of a picture, or between scenes, usually to indicate a jump in time and/or setting.

William Petersen and Jorja Fox in a scene from the seventh season of the popular television series CSI: Crime Scene Investigation

In a dissolve, one image fades out slowly while the next image fades in slowly. Halfway through, the two images become superimposed—that is, for a second or two, both images appear on the screen at the same time. Like fades, dissolves can indicate a jump in time, but usually suggest a deeper connection between one scene and the next than a fade.

CUTTING TO CONTINUITY

Editors spend the majority of their time cutting shots within a scene. The primary goal of scene editing is continuity—that is, putting shots together logically to render the action more or less realistically. Some directors, like Alfred Hitchcock, Steven Spielberg, and M. Night Shyamalan, are known for "editing in the camera," that is, for planning and shooting their scenes so carefully that large-scale editorial decision making is not required. Even these directors, however, need skilled editors to make their shots work on-screen.

"Cutting to continuity" simply means that cuts are smooth and any reduction of time and space is rendered unnoticeable by the viewer. A scene depicting a woman crossing a parking lot and opening a car door, for instance, might start with a long shot showing the woman walking up to the car, then cut to a closer shot of her arm reaching for the door handle. If edited properly, the viewer will not be aware that a few moments of the action have been removed to save screen time.

According to editor Karel Reisz, "the most elementary requirement of a smooth continuity is that the actions of two consecutive shots of a single scene should match. . . . [I]f a scene is shot from more than one angle, the background and positions of the players remain the same in each take."[1] In other words, the scene should flow without visual glitches.

Some aspects of continuity are dealt with right on the production set. During filming, the script supervisor makes sure that all the visual elements in a scene match from shot to shot. The script supervisor will note such things as what the actors were wearing in each shot, where props were located, and what actions the actors were engaged in while speaking lines of dialogue. For example, if an actress says a given line while drying her hands in Shot One, the script supervisor will make sure that the actress is drying her hands when the same line comes up again in Shot Four.

COVERAGE AND BEYOND

Continuity requires visual consistency within a scene. Unless it is being filmed in a single shot, the scene also needs to be shot from enough angles, or covered, to cut together well. If coverage is lacking, the rendered action may be confusing or disjointed. If the problem is identified while shooting is still going on, the editor will likely request that cutaway or insert shots be done. Cutaways are noncritical shots, often close-ups, that help link actions in a scene. Sometimes, however, the editor must find ways to compensate for inadequate coverage without the benefit of additional shooting.

> CUTAWAY—A shot, usually a close-up, that is used to break up an action sequence. Frequently used to cover a break in continuity or coverage. A cutaway does not focus on details of the shot before or after it but cuts away from the action.

In classic editing, as developed by D. W. Griffith, coverage footage is cut together in such a way as to make continuity easy. The long master shot (establishing shot) introduces the setting at the beginning of a scene. Medium shots of the actors, including two-shots and over-the-shoulder and reverse angle shots, come next, followed by close-ups.

As the scene progresses, the editor will go back and forth between medium and close-up shots and may return to the establishing shot. The goal of the "Griffith formula," as it is sometimes called, is to bring the viewer into the scene as clearly and quickly as possible.

> MASTER SHOT— A single continuous shot that contains the action of an entire scene.

As useful and as used as the Griffith formula is, many scenes require a different approach, especially those designed around a moving camera. Whatever the approach, editors usually sift through a number of different shots and takes before hitting on the right combination. As

> TWO-SHOT — A medium shot featuring two actors.

veteran editor Thelma Schoonmaker (*Raging Bull*, *The Departed*) noted,

> You take one shot and connect to another shot, and if you don't feel that little jolt of electricity that happens when you cut two shots together you know it's not working. So you reject that shot and you try another one. And you keep doing that until you arrive at a shape for the battle because the battle didn't have a predefined shape to it. Make sure things aren't dragging too long.[2]

Beyond the basic visual requirements described above, good editing demands that cuts make dramatic sense. Since cutting implies juxtapositioning—placing two elements next to each other—editors always have to consider how the pieces flow together. According to Edward Dmytryk's first rule of editing, cuts should never be dramatically arbitrary—a cut for a cut's sake—but should be made for *good* reason.

> As a sequence is being cut, the cutter should know where a particular setup most effectively presents the information needed for that particular part of the scene. In other words, he will stay with a shot as long as that shot is the one which best delivers the required information and cut to another shot only when the new cut will better serve the purposes of the scene, whether because the size is more effective, the composition is more suitable, or the interpretation is superior.[3]

CUTTING ON ACTION

The fundamental goal of conventional cutting—the actual splicing together of two pieces of film—is to make the transition from one shot to the next as undetectable as possible. "The exact cutting point," according to Edward Dmytryk, "would depend on the cutter's sense of proper timing. All exceptional editors have this sense to an exceptional degree."[4]

Cuts are never invisible—if a viewer makes a point of looking for them, they are easy to spot. When the editor does his or her job well, however, the viewer will remain happily unaware of editing. According to Karel Reisz, "Making a smooth cut means joining two shots in such a way that the transition does not create a noticeable jerk and the spectator's illusion of seeing a continuous piece of action is not interrupted."[5]

The easiest way to avoid the "bad," or noticeable, edit is to cut on action. Movement within the frame causes blurring, and blurring distracts the viewer's eye. Even the stillest shot contains some blur, but editors usually look for obvious motion when picking cut points.

According to editor/teacher Richard D. Pepperman, "If shots are joined at frames of extreme action—and greatest blur—the eye might fail to spot the cut."[6] In the earlier example of the woman and the car door, the editor would likely cut during the act of reaching. The moving hand would create sufficient blur to distract the eye temporarily. Waiting to cut until her fingers were already on the handle, or cutting a second before she started to reach out, on the other hand, would minimize the blur and result in an awkward cut.

Picking which frame to cut on within the blur is a matter of trial and error and the editor's instincts. Pepperman notes that smooth cutting requires a balance of blur between one shot and the next: "There are instances when a cut is disturbing because the movement (however slight), effects a trifling of blur in the Outgoing frame that exceeds (or is less than) the blur in the Incoming frame."[7] In other words, if the first shot, or outgoing, ends on extreme movement and the second, or incoming, begins on less motion, the cut will be jarring to the viewer.

SCREEN DIRECTION

Another aspect of continuity that editors must always be aware of is screen direction. In his book *The Technique of Film and Video Editing*, editor/historian Ken Dancyger notes that in order to avoid confusion, "a strict left-to-right or right-to-left pattern must be maintained. When a character goes out to buy groceries, he may leave his house heading toward the right side of the frame. . . . If he exited to the right, he must travel left to right until he gets to the store."[8] If a character walks toward the right side of the frame in one shot, he should enter the next shot from the left.

According to an editorial rule of thumb, the outgoing shot in the scene described above should cut out as the actor's eyes pass the edge of the picture and the incoming shot should cut in six frames (a quarter of a second) before the actor's eyes appear in the next setup. Editors follow this rule because it takes about a quarter of a second for a viewer's eyes to move from one side of the frame to the other. During that quarter of a second, vision is blurred and the viewer does not register jumps in action.

Maintaining consistent screen direction can also help viewers stay visually oriented during complex action scenes. Directional consistency is particularly important for depicting battles, sports action, and any scene in which opposing groups face off against one another.

RHYTHM AND TEMPO

Sergei Eisenstein was not only expert at juxtaposition, but he also understood the importance of tempo in editing. Eisenstein was the first director to cut a scene to the beats of a music score, and his editing was known for its rhythmic precision. Although it is rare today to cut films to a precise musical beat, directors are nonetheless keenly aware of tempo when they are overseeing the editing of a picture. According to Martin Scorsese, "It's the editor who orchestrates the rhythm of the images, and that is the rhythm of the dialogue, and

This scene from Eisenstein's Battleship Potemkin *(1925) is a good example of the director's use of juxtaposition.*

of course the rhythm of the music. For me, the editor is like a musician, and often a composer."[9]

SETTING TEMPO

Some shots, like long traveling shots, set their own tempo. Most shots, however, must be cut with others to achieve a desired tempo. The easiest way for an editor to affect the pacing of a scene is by shortening or expanding the time it takes to depict a particular activity. In addition to cutting out small bits of action from one shot to the next, editors can use commonly understood visual cues to imply offscreen action.

For example, if in one scene a woman peers out a living room window and waves at a passerby on the sidewalk, then in the following scene, the woman appears outside talking to the passerby, the audience will assume the two scenes are taking place more or less continuously. The viewer does not need to see the woman exiting the house and walking over to the passerby to understand the connection between the two actions.

In some instances, however, a scene may benefit from lingering on a shot, showing an entire action, or from repeating certain moments. In general, because they contain more visual information, long shots require more screen time than do close-ups, as do any shots that present new or unexpected information. If a scene requires that two characters observe the same object at the same time and register opposite reactions, the editor will likely include shots showing each actor looking at and reacting to the object. Screen time will then double real time.

The famous closing shot of Carol Reed's *The Third Man* (1949), which was filmed with a telephoto lens, lasts over a minute and merely shows the heroine walking down a long path, past the rejected hero and out of frame. The physical activity of the scene could have been rendered in a few on-screen seconds, but by staying on the entire action, the

Alida Valli portraying Anna Schmidt in a scene from Carol Reed's The Third Man *(1949).*

sadness and finality of the moment are more deeply conveyed.

Depicting an action in a single long take, instead of mixing a master shot with medium shots and close-ups, tends to slow the pace of a scene. In his book *Making Movies*, director Sidney Lumet observes, "The more cuts, the faster the tempo will seem."[10] Reisz adds, "When a sustained impression of rapid action is desired, it is often better to achieve this through *varying* the pace rather than by keeping to a constant maximum rate. . . . The *acceleration* of tempo evokes a much greater feeling of fast activity than would a constant maximum rate of cutting."[11]

In addition to fixing the tempo for each scene, the editor has to be aware of the overall pace of the film, the scene-to-scene rhythm. A thirty-second television commercial can be cut to the same tempo (usually fast), but not a full-length film. Lumet notes that "if a picture is edited in the same tempo for its entire length, it will *feel* much longer. It doesn't matter if five cuts per minute or five cuts every ten minutes are being used. . . . In other words, it's the *change* in tempo that we feel, not the tempo itself."[12]

EDITING ACTORS AND DIALOGUE

For most editors the most important ingredient in a film, besides the script itself, is the acting. Editor Leander Sales (*Malcolm X*) loves to cut performances because for him it is like "watching the 'human' being born."[13]

Editing Dialogue in *The Aviator*

Multiple Academy Award winner Thelma Schoonmaker
is probably best known for her work on the 1980
boxing film *Raging Bull*, directed by Martin Scorsese.
Schoonmaker first met Scorsese in the early 1960s
when the director was a film student at New York
University. She helped him out on a student production,
and a special collaborative bond was formed. Since
Raging Bull, Schoonmaker has edited every one of
Scorsese's films, including the 2004 release *The Aviator*,
a biopic about brilliant, eccentric millionaire Howard
Hughes.

Schoonmaker worked closely with Scorsese on *The
Aviator*, helping to shape the three-hour-plus story into
a consistent whole. Schoonmaker's Oscar-winning
editing is remarkable for its many spectacular flying
scenes and scenes showing Hughes's descent into
mental illness. Less noticeable but equally impressive is
Schoonmaker's editing on the film's many long dialogue
scenes.

One such scene occurs approximately two-and-a-half
hours into the film. After revealing to his competitor,
Juan Trippe (Alec Baldwin), his plans to begin cross-
Atlantic flights with his new fleet of TWA airplanes,
Howard Hughes (Leonardo DiCaprio) is called to appear

before the U.S. Senate. Hughes has been accused by Trippe's friend Senator Brewster (Alan Alda) of defrauding the government of $56 million in wartime airplane contracts. Previously Brewster, who stands to profit if Trippe's airline becomes the only trans-Atlantic carrier in America, had tried to pressure Hughes into backing out of his plans by threatening to prosecute him publicly.

Having ignored Brewster's threats, Hughes is called before his Senate committee in the summer of 1947. The two scenes depicting the Senate hearings last about ten minutes. Sandwiched in between is a four-minute scene showing Hughes taking off in California on a test flight of his enormous Hercules (Spruce Goose) airplane.

Courtroom-type scenes like this one are always a challenge for filmmakers because they are physically constrained and filled with dialogue. In *The Aviator*, Schoonmaker used various devices to keep the pace and tension of the Senate hearings going, while at the same time conveying the personal drama behind Hughes's appearance.

The goal of the sequence is to show Hughes triumphing over Brewster, beating him at his own game, in his own territory. In order to win the battle, Hughes must overcome his fears long enough to take charge of the hearing. At this point in the story, Hughes has become deeply disturbed and can barely function in the everyday world. During the first day of the hearing, he appears tense and distracted, while Brewster is calm and in control. By the end of the sequence, however, Hughes is the one asking the questions and putting Brewster on the defensive.

How does the editing help realize the sequence's goal? During the first minutes, Schoonmaker highlights Hughes's troubled state by cutting in many close-ups of the bright lights and newsreel cameras recording the hearing, objects that cause Hughes great anxiety. Also included are shots looking back at Hughes from the camera's point of view and close-ups of his hand tugging at his pants leg under the hearing table. These frequent visual interruptions intensify the spoken exchange and create a nervous, frantic feel. As Hughes starts to get the upper hand with Brewster, however, Schoonmaker abandons the cutaways and stays focused on the two actors.

Throughout the sequence, Schoonmaker keeps the dialogue moving by extending the speech of the outgoing shot into the visuals of the incoming shot. Frequently during the sequence, the voice of one actor continues on the soundtrack while the picture cuts to show the reaction of the other actor. Instead of remaining on the actor until the end of his speech and then cutting to a reaction shot of the listener, Schoonmaker presents the reaction while the speech is still going on. This technique allows Schoonmaker to cut more often and thereby increase the pace of the exchange.

On a broader structural level, Schoonmaker breaks up the sequence by cutting away to the Hercules launch in California. As noted in the film, the flight actually takes place months after the hearing. According to Schoonmaker, she and Scorsese deviated from the film's chronology in order to make an important thematic connection:

> The intercutting of it [the hearing] with the Hercules flight scene was a revolutionary change. Originally, the Hercules was going to take off in one chunk. . . . We started experimenting with various ways of intercutting the Senate. Eventually we ended up with only one. It's kind of a bizarre intercut; it's very weird. But when you go back and see Hughes talk about the Hercules, you now know what he's talking about more than before we intercut it. It's stronger.[14]

In the book *The Conversations*, Walter Murch compares actors to pieces of sculpture:

> In the course of editing, you look at all the material for the scene, over and over again. Your decisions about timing, about where to cut a certain shot and what shot to go to next, all those things, are dependent on an intuitive understanding of the actors. You have to have, and you do acquire, a deep, deep knowledge of the actors. . . . You are studying them the way a sculptor studies a piece of marble before deciding to chisel it—here. So I have to know all the hidden veins and strengths and weaknesses of the rock that I'm working with, in order to know where best to put the chisel.[15]

Occasionally actors fail to deliver and the editor must work around their performance. Longtime editor Billy Weber (*Top Gun*, *Thin Red Line*) firmly believes that good performances can be made in the editing room, often by eliminating dialogue. "It's amazing how a look is worth a thousand words. . . . That's especially true when you're cutting a scene and the actor's not too good, but they look good. They look thoughtful, or they look serious, or hurt, or happy. Sometimes it's more important to do the look than the dialogue."[16]

Editing performances often comes down to the cutting of dialogue. According to Weber, cutting dialogue is the most time-consuming element of editing as well as the most difficult, but artistically rewarding element. In action scenes—car chases, gun battles, space travel, etc.—Weber notes, the director and editor can make up the "ground rules" because it is unlikely the audience has firsthand knowledge of the activity. "If two people are having an argument everyone knows what that feels like, everyone knows what that looks like. So it's much easier to find a false moment in a scene like that, than it is in an action scene."[17] Scenes dominated by dialogue frequently are shot and cut as a series of back-and-forth medium over-the-shoulder shots, or as a medium two-shot, in which both actors appear together in the same frame. The dialogue exchange may be introduced by an establishing shot, indicating location and other pertinent details, and be punctuated by close-ups. Generally the speaking actor stays on-screen during the delivery of his or her lines, but sometimes the editor might cut to a shot of the listener, especially if the listener's reaction is vital to the scene's effectiveness. Making dialogue believable involves finding the right rhythm, or beats, for each line. Just as screenwriters use trial and error to come up with dialogue rhythms for their characters, editors go back and forth with cuts to find the best start and end points for lines. For example, editors decide whether to keep the speaking actor's dramatic pause intact, or have the listener jump in with a response.

IN THE EDITING ROOM

As with all elements of filmmaking, the editing process begins with the screenplay. Typically editors enter the process during preproduction, before shooting on a picture begins. The editor will discuss the script with the director, voicing concerns and asking questions. In some instances, an editor's analysis of a script will determine whether he or she will be hired for a particular production.

When interviewing prospective editors, director Jon Turteltaub (*Cool Runnings*, *National Treasure*) looks for someone who understands "the heart of the script." Sometimes an editor can change or enhance the way a director approaches the script. Before hiring Bruce Green to edit *Cool Runnings*, for example, Turteltaub asked him what the story was about. "He told me, 'It's about dignity.' I had known what kind of film I wanted to make, but the word itself had not occurred to me. I thought, 'That's right, it is about dignity,' and that helped set the tone for the film."[1]

Billy Weber contends that a director hires an editor strictly for his or her opinions, especially when it comes to storytelling. "You're not being hired for how well you make a cut from a close-up to a wide shot. You're being hired for your observations and your opinions."[2]

Walter Murch says, "When I'm considering a project, I read the script, take notes, type them up, and give them to the director. I would include both what I think is good about the script—what attracted me to it—and where I think there may be room for improvement. . . . There may be something too long or repetitive, or maybe the script gave me some idea about transposing two scenes. Already, I'm kind of editing."[3]

THE EDITING TEAM

Although most productions employ only one editor, it is not unusual, especially on big productions, to see two or three editors listed in the credits. The editor listed first is the lead editor. In addition to cutting a portion of the footage, the lead editor oversees editing on the entire production. He or she views and approves scenes cut by others.

Dmytryk describes the lead editor this way: "At the top of the scale is the *creative editor*, the person with an understanding of dramatic structure, a keen sense of timing, a compulsion to seek out the scene's hidden values—values which even the writer and the director may not have clearly grasped (believe me, it does happen!)—and a mastery of the technical skills needed to bring all these talents to bear on the film he edits."[4]

Helping the editor are assistants and apprentices. Years ago, editors were required to work as apprentices and assistants for a certain number of years before they could be hired as full-fledged editors. No such requirements exist today, but most editors spend some time as apprentices and assistants before becoming an editor. The "assistant team" usually consists of a first assistant, second assistant, and an apprentice.

Using a computerized system, apprentice and assistant editors catalogue and keep track of all footage that comes into the editing room. During production, they act as liaisons between the editing room and the various processing laboratories. They coordinate and take notes during the screening of footage shot each day, and they organize and maintain reports from the camera, sound, and script departments. During postproduction, they clean, measure, and recut footage as needed. They also set up screenings of edited scenes.

POSTPRODUCTION—
The phase of film production that occurs after principal photography has been completed.

Sometimes experienced assistants are permitted to do more creative work. The editor might ask them for artistic feedback, or to cut temporary sound effects and music. Occasionally they edit entire scenes. Once picture editing has been completed, the assistant oversees the creation of such optical effects as fades and dissolves. He or she continues to work with the sound department, and in some cases oversees the final editorial stages of postproduction.

Once filming starts, editors and their assistants assemble the raw footage as it is completed and sent in from the set or location. Thanks to computer technology, editors can now view and cut this footage, called dailies, within hours of shooting, "fresh from the set." While screening dailies, the editor chooses takes and makes notes about coverage or other shooting details, such as lighting. The editor then removes the selected takes and cuts them together according to the director's original shot order. Takes that are not selected are called outtakes.

From this initial assembly, the editor begins to shape the footage into a rough cut. The editor screens the footage scene by scene to determine the effectiveness of the shot selection and structure. As it is put together, the editor and director ask, is the scene clear? Is the coverage adequate? Does the scene advance the story? Are the performances convincing? If necessary, the order of scenes can be changed, or a scene can be reedited to change the point of view or dramatic emphasis, or to compensate for a poor acting performance.

> ROUGH CUT—
> The crudely edited total footage of a film.

Once the film's scene-by-scene structure has been worked out, the editor begins to polish and tighten the film. This last stage of picture editing is called the fine cut. The primary concern of the fine cut is to adjust the tempo, or pace, of the movie. At this point, filming has been completed, and director and editor are sitting together in the editing room, going over every second of the picture.

> FINE CUT—The final stage of editing a film.

EDITING FOR TELEVISION

Where cinematic art is concerned, editing for television is a lot like editing for feature movies. TV editors work with the same equipment and materials as feature editors and have the same artistic objective—putting a good story up on the screen. Because of tighter schedules and smaller budgets, however, television editors rarely have as much time as feature editors to assemble their product. Editorial teams are also smaller on television shows than on features, and assistants have fewer opportunities for creative editing. To meet deadlines, editors and their assistants are often expected to work on more than one episode at a time.

On the plus side, however, editors working in television have more creative flexibility than those who work on features. It is not unusual for a television editor to cut a show's sound and music as well as its visuals. Often on a TV series, editing facilities are located next to the shooting facilities, and the editorial team enjoys greater interaction with the production crew than most feature-film teams.

As with writers and directors, editors who work on TV series must adhere to a particular show's style and content. On the hit show *Lost*, for example, editors have to cut carefully to maintain the show's mystery and avoid revealing too much visual information. The show's complex narrative, with its

Some of the cast in a scene from the popular television series Lost

many characters, story lines, and flashbacks, also presents them with a special editorial challenge. As assistant editor Lance Stubblefield explains, "The story is extremely intricate, so we often need to go back to old daily footage in order to fill in missing pieces of the story."[5]

While cutting the series *Night Stalker*, editor Christopher Cooke had a different concern. Cooke had to be mindful that, unlike *Lost*, every episode of *Night Stalker* was self-contained, that is, it had its own beginning, middle, and end. In an interview conducted during the show's production, Cooke noted, "Each week we try to tell a creepy, scary or unusual story with feature film aesthetics and a fun-loving touch."[6]

According to editor Brianna London, one of the biggest editorial challenges on the medical drama *Grey's Anatomy* "is the music, which features new, innovative, breakout bands. . . . It's fun to find the music and place it for the appropriate emotional high point of the scene."[7]

Another concern for television editors, of course, are the commercial breaks, which impose a rigid structure on the story's spine. As editor Tina Hirsch (*Independence Day*, *West Wing*) pointed out in a recent interview: "Act One has to be a certain length. Act Two has to be a certain length. When you come to the end of the editing process in television, after finely crafting a piece of material, you might realize that the show is still 10 seconds too long. 'But it's just

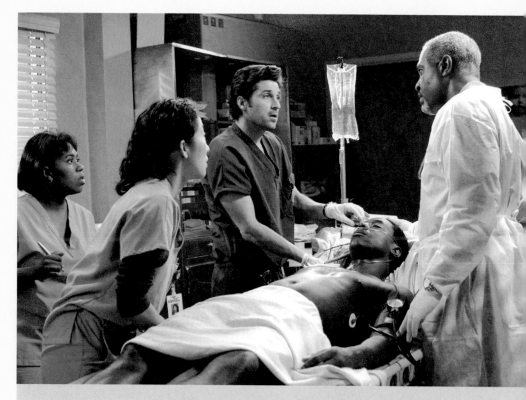

A *scene from the television medical drama* Grey's Anatomy

right,' you think to yourself! 'How can we take 10 seconds out without making it awkward?' Somehow you always manage to."[8]

Because television screens are smaller than movie screens, TV editors need to rely more on medium shots and close-ups than do feature editors. Visual details that would be noticeable in a long shot on the big screen would be lost in a similar shot on the small screen. TV shows usually have more dialogue than movies.

The Linear vs. Nonlinear Debate

Films cut on Moviolas are edited in a linear fashion. That is, one shot is placed after another to create a single, very long strand of film. Computerized editing, like the Avid system, is done in a nonlinear fashion. With nonlinear editing, shots and scenes can be ordered and reordered the same way words and sentences can be cut and pasted in a computer word program. Now that nonlinear editing has become the norm within the industry, many editors who began their careers on Moviolas have expressed varying opinions about the two systems. Below are some of the pros and cons of each, as observed by industry pros:

Walter Murch: I think there are only two areas where something is missing [in nonlinear editing]. When you actually had to make the cut physically on film, you naturally tended to think more about what you were about to do. Which—in the right proportion—is a good thing to do. The cut is a kind of sacramental moment. When I was in grade school they made us write our essays in ink for the same reason. Pencil was too easy to erase. The other "missing" advantage to linear editing was the natural integration of repeatedly scanning through rolls of film to get to a shot you wanted. Inevitably, before you ever got there, you found something that was better than what you had in mind. With random access, you immediately get what you want. Which may not be what you need.[9]

Dede Allen: . . . the greatest disadvantage [of nonlinear editing] I can think of is that you don't screen your material as much as you used to. . . . In film [linear], by screening more often, you had a much better overall perspective. . . . Maybe that happens on an Avid too, but I don't think it happens as much because the process is faster and it can make us more impatient, less willing to take the time to continually view a scene or a cut in context.[10]

Andrew Mondshein: It seems fairly clear that the history of film is an evolving art form rooted in technological developments. Of course, with any new technology there's both a nostalgia for the old way and some real fundamental process changes that arguably are not always for the better. In the instance of non-linear editing, I'm a firm believer that the positives far outweigh the negatives.[11]

The ability to edit dialogue efficiently and effectively is key to a TV editor's success.

FROM THE MOVIOLA TO FINAL CUT PRO

The first machine designed to edit motion pictures was called the Moviola. Its inventor, Iwan Serrurier, originally conceived the Moviola as a home projector. The projector, built in 1923, was very expensive, however, and Serrurier had a hard time marketing it. Then an editor at silent movie star Douglas Fairbanks's studio showed him how film shots were assembled. Until that time, editors had to pass strips of film by hand over a light well, make a cut, and then run each cut through a projector to see if the edit worked. The editor asked Serrurier if his projector could be modified so that cuts could be made and viewed on the same machine. Over a weekend, Serrurier made the changes to his projector. He removed the lamp house and projection lens, turned the machine upside down, and attached a viewing lens. He also attached a hand crank to the projector's intermittent movement mechanism, which he had adapted from a clock. The editors at Fairbanks loved it, and in 1924, the Moviola editing machine was born.

Today, a majority of films and TV shows are edited on compact computerized systems. Although the first crude version of an electronic editing system appeared in the early 1970s, the first feature film to

Actor Gerard Depardieu reviews film through a Moviola with a film editor in 2001.

be cut with an electronic system, called Montage, was Sidney Lumet's 1986 release *Power*, edited by Andrew Mondshein.

The type of editing technology used today emerged in the late 1980s, with the development of the Avid system. Based on Apple's Macintosh computer platform, Avid software included the Media Composer, the first system with timeline editing and clip bins. Other editing systems, including Microsoft's Final Cut Pro, were released in the 1990s, but Avid remains the system of choice among professional editors.

SOUND EDITING

4

Although the term "film editing" generally refers to the cutting of visuals, no movie would make it to the screen without sound editing. Picture and sound editing are complementary arts, but compared to picture editing, sound editing is a relatively new art.

Sound film did not become standard until about 1929, and the manipulation of movie sound for dramatic purposes did not become a routine part of filmmaking until much later. Films like Alfred Hitchcock's *Blackmail* (1929), Ernest Schoedsack and Merian C. Cooper's *King Kong* (1933), and Orson Welles's *Citizen Kane* (1941) used sound creatively. Most filmmakers during this period, however, focused only on making the dialogue audible.

Movie sound is generally divided into three elements: dialogue, music, and effects. Effects consist of any sound that is not speech or music. During production, sound recordists, or mixers, record and mix dialogue as it is spoken by the actors. Along with the actors' words, mixers also record noises—birds, cars, airplanes, etc.—that may or may not show up in the final film. Sometimes mixers record ambient noises—sounds associated with a given location—separate from the performances.

Sound in the earliest "talkies" was recorded separately on a phonograph record and synchronized later with the filmed images. This process is called sound-on-disc. Optical sound, a sound-on-film process, eventually became the industry standard. The sound-on-film process converts recorded sound into a signal that can be photographed along with the film in the camera. The photographed signal is later separated into tracks.

Each track contains its own type of sound—all dialogue of a particular actor, all effects, etc. Individual tracks can be manipulated, or mixed, to create a specific effect or correction. The more tracks a film contains, the more subtle and sophisticated the mix will be. For the final film, tracks are rejoined and mixed together in a mixing session. Good mixing ensures that all sounds serve the dramatic needs of the scene as intended.

Early optical recordings could only be broken down into a maximum of eight tracks. Although inexpensive and simple to use, optical recordings were noisy and monotonal. They lacked texture and depth.

In the 1950s, magnetic recording began to replace optical recording as the movie sound system of choice. With magnetic technology, movie sound mixers could create stereo recordings that were cleaner and crisper than optical recordings. Magnetic recordings were expensive, cumbersome, and fragile, however.

The late 1960s and 1970s saw the emergence of Dolby sound technology. Dolby technology enabled filmmakers to return to cheaper, sturdier optical recording by reducing significantly unwanted noise. The 1971 Stanley Kubrick picture *A Clockwork Orange* was the first major film released in Dolby.

Today most movie sound is recorded digitally. Digital sound actually represents a return to the sound-on-disc format. Instead of the sound being stored on film, digital sound is stored on computer discs. Digital recordings can contain as many as a thousand tracks, though forty to sixty tracks are typical.

POSTPRODUCTION

Because it is the most natural sounding, directors generally prefer dialogue that is recorded live on a set or location. Often, however, some or all of a scene's dialogue needs to be rerecorded due to excess background noise (airplanes, for instance) or a problematic performance. On average, 30 percent of a feature film's dialogue ends up being rerecorded in a sound studio.

A scene from Stanley Kubrick's A Clockwork Orange *(1971), the first film to be released in Dolby sound.*

Rerecording of dialogue is done in postproduction by an ADR (automatic dialogue replacement) editor. The actor will screen the scene over and over again, while listening to the original soundtrack on headphones. Speaking in sync to match the visuals, the actor will then rerecord dialogue.

THE SOUND EDITING CREW

The sound editing crew on a typical Hollywood movie is large and diverse. On most of today's films the lead picture editor is responsible for hiring the sound editing crew, and many picture editors work with the same sound editors movie after movie. Because a film's sound has to synch up with and complement the visuals, sound editors must collaborate closely with picture editors. Often their editing rooms are next to one another to allow for frequent "conferencing."

In addition to editing dialogue and noises recorded during production, sound editors are responsible for adding prerecorded and live sound effects as well as background music to the soundtrack. On many Hollywood productions, sound editors are assigned to work exclusively in one area—dialogue, effects, or music.

Some sound effects can be found in a sound library—a prerecorded collection of frequently used sounds, such as birds and traffic. Others are recorded live specifically for the production. Certain sound effects are created on a stage by foley artists (named after effects pioneer Jack Foley). Using a variety of objects and techniques, foley artists add noises to the soundtrack that the production recordist may have deliberately excluded during filming. Common foley sounds include squeaks, clothing rustles, footsteps, and door slams. Without these everyday noises, movies would sound flat and unnatural. "Foleying" helps filmmakers create a textured, realistic world while ensuring that the dialogue can still be heard.

> FOLEY — The recording of custom sound effects. The term comes from the name of its inventor, Jack Foley.

Sound designer is a relatively new position that straddles all areas of movie sound, including editing. Like cinematographers, sound designers confer with the director early on about an overall approach to a movie's soundtrack. Sound designers study the film's script, looking for ways to convey character and story elements through sound. They are involved in every phase of production, from shooting to final edit.

MUSIC

Like sound, music is yet another filmmaking element that can be manipulated for effect. A few scores consist solely of non-original music—music, often popular songs, written before the film. Director Stanley Kubrick used only non-original orchestral music for his memorable *2001: A Space Odyssey* (1968) score. Some movie scores, like that for *Star*

Mark Hamill, Carrie Fisher, and Harrison Ford (left to right) star as Luke Skywalker, Princess Leia, and Han Solo, respectively, in a scene from the blockbuster film Star Wars *(1977).*

Wars (1977), are wholly original, with every note being composed just for the film. Other films, like *Garden State* (2004), use a combination of original and non-original music.

It is the job of the music editor to incorporate the recorded musical score into the soundtrack. The music editor works closely with the film composer and/or music supervisor and director to document decisions about the placement, timing, length, and type of music to be used throughout a project.

Ben Burtt and
The Sounds of *Star Wars*

Along with Walter Murch, Ben Burtt is one of the most accomplished sound editor-designers working in Hollywood. He has won numerous awards, including Oscars for *Raiders of the Lost Ark* (1989) and *E.T.* (1982).

Burtt, who earned a degree in physics, cemented his reputation early on, collaborating with George Lucas on *Star Wars* (1977) soon after graduating. In a recent online question-and-answer session, Burtt revealed how he created some of his memorable *Star Wars* sound effects.

Lightsabers: I remembered a sound of an interlock motor on the old film projectors at the USC Cinema Department (I had been a projectionist there). The motors made a musical "hum" which I felt immediately would complement the image in the painting. I recorded that motor, and a few days later I had a broken microphone cable that caused my recorder to accidentally pick up the buzz from the back of my TV picture tube. I recorded that buzz, and mixed it with the hum of the projector motor. Together these sounds became the basis for all the lightsabers.

Chewbacca: Mostly bear, with a dash of walrus, dog, and lion thrown in.

Sith Hologram: The Sith hologram tonality is partly made on an electronic synthesizer. . . . I also mixed in some short wave radio sounds that you can hear between broadcasting stations. This is one of my favorite sources of sound. Finally I added a very very slowed down sound of a jet plane firing a Vulcan Cannon, an electronically driven machine gun that fires 100 bullets per second.

Roars of the acklay, nexu, and reek: Some dolphins and pigs were used, but actually a main component for both the acklay and the reek were made by dragging a huge wooden palette across the sound stage floor in Sydney.[1]

During dubbing sessions the music editor then inserts the recorded music—score, live vocals, songs—into the film at predetermined points, called cues.

THE ART OF SOUND EDITING

Even more than picture editing, good sound editing should go unnoticed by the audience. Movie sound should not only clearly convey necessary information, like dialogue, but should also contribute to the theme, tone, and mood of the piece. According to Ken Dancyger, "Because of the number of tracks used, the sound edit is even more elaborate and requires many more decisions than the picture edit. Because a wrong decision can undermine the visuals so readily, the sound edit is complex and critical. Without an effective sound track, the visuals will not succeed."[2]

Sound designers and/or editors, like picture editors, always consider the story's premise when making decisions. They will devise an overall approach to a film's sound based on the needs of the story. Just as they have a certain visual "look," films can have a sound "look," or style. Science fiction and fantasy movies like the *Lord of the Rings* trilogy (2001–2004) tend to have dense soundtracks, filled with effects that help make their imaginary worlds come alive. Sometimes the visual style and the sound style complement each other. Clint Eastwood's 1988 biography of jazzman Charlie

Parker, *Bird*, for example, favors a cool, blue look and a cool jazz score.

According to Oscar-winning sound editor Randy Thom (*Polar Express*, *Harry Potter and the Goblet of Fire*) scenes with a strong point of view can benefit especially from thoughtful sound design. Thom says, "The photography, the blocking of actors, the production design, art direction, editing, and dialogue have been set up such that we, the audience, are experiencing the action more or less through the point of view of one, or more, of the characters in the sequence. Since what we see and hear is being filtered through their consciousness, what they hear can give us lots of information about who they are and what they are feeling."[3]

Movie sound, its dialogue, effects, and music, serves a number of dramatic purposes.

- First and foremost, sound helps establish a believable cinematic world. Whether the story is taking place on a contemporary high school campus, or a planet in a faraway galaxy, the setting needs a consistent, identifiable palette of sounds. Although specific sounds often escape the audience's notice, the absence of sound or inappropriate or poor sound compromises the film's credibility.

- Like pictures, sounds help create point of view. To achieve subjectivity, certain sounds can be brought out, while others can be muted or silenced. In the 2004 film *Ray*, for example, sounds play a big part in conveying the visionless world of singer Ray Charles. By

Inge Landgut and Peter Lorre in a scene from the classic Fritz Lang film, M *(1931)*

emphasizing particular noises on the soundtrack, like water and chimes, the film allows viewers to get inside the character's head, even while they are seeing what Charles cannot.

- Sounds help define characters. When repeated, sounds can become associated with a particular character and can remind audiences of key events. In Fritz Lang's classic 1931 movie *M*, for example, a serial child killer is identified by a particular tune he whistles when he is stalking his victims.

- Sounds underline a character's emotional state. During one fight scene in his 1980 boxing picture *Raging Bull*, director Martin Scorsese and sound designer Frank Warner slowed down the sound of the fighters' punches to show the increasing exhaustion of main character Jake La Motta. Warner also used the harsh sound of reporters' popping flashbulbs to suggest Jake's vulnerability as a public figure.

- Sounds help establish a setting or time period. The clacking of a horse's hooves on cobblestones, for example, will immediately suggest a pre-twentieth century, urban setting. Chirping crickets and wind suggest an outdoor, rural setting.

- Sounds also convey shifts in time and place. Music in particular can be very effective at indicating time changes. In *The Aviator*, jumps in time are almost always accompanied by a musical selection from the new period. On the

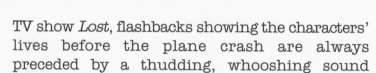

TV show *Lost*, flashbacks showing the characters' lives before the plane crash are always preceded by a thudding, whooshing sound effect.

- Like visual dissolves, sound dissolves, in which the first sounds of an incoming shot are heard over the image of the outgoing shot, help connect scenes, emotionally and thematically. Sound dissolves can also quicken a film's pace, as the audience begins to receive information about a change before the change occurs visually. In the congressional hearing sequence of *The Aviator*, the sound of Senator Brewster's voice introduces the shift from California back to Washington, D.C., for instance.

- Sounds heighten suspense. For example, in Alfred Hitchcock's *The Birds* (1963), the killer birds are heard cawing, on and off screen, prior to attacking. The audience comes to anticipate an attack every time a cawing noise is heard.

- Sounds can direct or misdirect the audience's attention. In a crowded courtroom scene the sound of a pounding gavel will direct the viewer toward the judge's bench. In horror movies, the sudden screeching of a cat in a dark place has become a clichéd way of fooling the audience and directing attention away from the scene's real danger.

- Background music conveys emotional states and tone. The type of music used in a scene can dramatically affect how the audience perceives the unfolding action. Dissonant music usually suggests lurking danger or emotional turmoil, for example, while upbeat music will suggest security and contentment.

- Musical themes associated with a particular character or setting can link scenes and provide clarity.

5 Putting It All Together: George Tomasini and *Psycho*

In 1959, executives at Paramount Pictures tried hard to discourage contracted producer-director Alfred Hitchcock from adapting a controversial pulp novel for the screen. The story was too gruesome in their opinion. The studio refused to pay Hitchcock's full salary and forced him to shoot the film on Universal's lot. Hitchcock persisted, however, and the resulting 1960 release, *Psycho*, not only made Hitchcock extremely wealthy, it changed horror movies forever.

American movie audiences had never seen anything quite like *Psycho*. In addition to breaking common rules of cinematic storytelling, the drama was truly shocking.

Despite the film's modest budget (around eight hundred thousand dollars), the film set box office records and was nominated for four Academy Awards. More recently, it was included on several "top 100" lists and in the American Film Institute's "100 Years" series, including "100 Movies" and "100 Thrills." The movie inspired three sequels, and in 1998, Gus Van Sant directed an almost exact, shot-by-shot remake. Many historians consider *Psycho* the father of the modern slasher film. Norman Bates, the movie's central character, set the standard for on-screen psychopaths. Bernard Herrmann's music score, which was unusual in that it was played entirely by stringed instruments, became synonymous with the movie horror genre. The film's editing also proved innovative and influential.

GEORGE TOMASINI

Psycho was edited by George Tomasini, who enjoyed a strong collaborative relationship with the director, Hitchcock. All together, Tomasini edited nine Hitchcock films, including *Vertigo*, *North by Northwest*, and *The Birds*. Although Hitchcock was known for his detailed preplanning and efficient shooting style, he relied on Tomasini for input and advice. "Mr. Hitchcock always gave George first cut," recalled Tomasini's widow in a recent interview. "He wanted to see his interpretation. Then they got down to the fine work."[1]

Tomasini's widow, Mary, recalled how Tomasini

> . . . would meet Mr. Hitchcock early in the morning to match film before they'd get started shooting, and then ran rushes [dailies] at night. But even at home, he [Tomasini] was thinking about a lot of things, trying to figure out how to make the film that he had come together. Sometimes you'd see him pacing the floor. He was off in a cutting room even when he was at home, trying to figure out how he was going to do certain things.[2]

Hilton Green, Hitchcock's assistant director on *Psycho*, stated in a video interview about the movie that Tomasini "had worked with Mr. H. for so long he really knew how to put it together. . . . Mr. Hitchcock was a frame cutter. He would cut down to frames where he knew precisely where he wanted that scene to be cut."[3] Like all good cutters, however, Tomasini understood the importance of precise timing, even in scenes that had been "edited in the camera."

THE STORY

Narratively *Psycho* presented many challenges. Robert Bloch's novel was inspired by the real-life killer Ed Gein, whose gruesome crimes made him a household name in the 1950s. Joseph Stefano adapted the novel for the screen, preserving its plot twists and trick ending. Prior to the film's release, Hitchcock went to elaborate lengths to ensure that the various story surprises remained secret.

Director Alfred Hitchcock and actor Anthony Perkins (left to right) on the set of Hitchcock's 1960 film, Psycho

One of the surprises involved the movie's star performer, Janet Leigh. The film opens with Leigh's character, Marion Crane, stealing forty thousand dollars in cash from her employer in Phoenix, Arizona. Marion takes the money so that she can marry her longtime boyfriend, Sam Loomis (John Gavin), a financially strapped hardware store owner who lives in the small California town of Fairvale. Instead of depositing the cash at the bank, Marion drives out of town with it.

After a nerve-racking encounter with a California highway patrolman, Marion trades cars at a used car dealer. That night during a fierce rainstorm, Marion misses the turnoff to Fairvale and decides to stop at the deserted Bates Motel. The motel's kind but odd proprietor, Norman Bates (Anthony Perkins), puts her in a room next to his office and offers to make sandwiches for her.

While nervously settling into her room, Marion hears Norman arguing about her with his mother in a large old house behind the motel. Later in the motel office, Norman apologizes to Marion, explaining that his mother is an unhappy invalid. Over sandwiches, Marion chats with Norman about life and, without revealing her crime, resolves to return the money the next day.

Marion returns to her room, where Norman watches her through a peephole as she undresses. Moments after Marion begins to take a shower, a shadowy knife-wielding woman bursts into the bathroom. Plunging the knife over and over, the woman stabs Marion to death. Norman then discovers Marion's body and, cursing his mother, cleans the bathroom of her blood. Norman places the body in the trunk of Marion's car and submerges it in a nearby swamp.

The death of Marion—Janet Leigh—forty-seven minutes into the film was the movie's first big surprise. Hitchcock gambled that viewers would be so involved in the story by that time that they would happily keep watching, despite losing their point-of-view character. Hitchcock's bet paid off.

BREAKING IT DOWN— THE SHOWER SCENE

Psycho's "shower scene" has long been considered one of the most stunning examples of suspenseful movie editing ever created, and one of the most influential scenes in cinema history. For decades, film students have studied it. Scholars have argued about it, and filmmakers have copied and parodied it. Entire books have been dedicated to analyzing it. One Internet site even offers users the chance to edit their own version of the scene.

Hitchcock originally conceived the scene as a montage sequence. Saul Bass, who at the time of the movie's release was well-known as a title designer, worked with Hitchcock to create a detailed storyboard of the sequence prior to shooting. Hitchcock reportedly told Bass that he intended to

The shower scene in Hitchcock's Psycho *(above) remains one of the most iconic scenes in cinema history.*

shoot and cut the scene "staccato," or in an abrupt, disconnected fashion.

In an interview contained in the book *Alfred Hitchcock and the Making of Psycho*, Bass described the shower scene as a "series of repetitive images in which there was a lot of motion but little activity . . . the movement was very narrow and the amount of activity to get you there was very intense."[4]

To some extent, Hitchcock's staccato approach evolved out of necessity. At the time of the film's production, on-screen nudity and extreme violence were prohibited by the censors. To avoid exposing too much flesh, Hitchcock and Bass chose shots that offered a limited view of Leigh's naked body. Instead of eye-level long and medium shots, Hitchcock and Bass designed the scene with odd-angled medium shots and close-ups. These shots were then chopped up into many pieces, making it all but impossible for the average viewer to notice actual nudity or knife stabs.

Although Hitchcock's initial motivation may have been to dodge the censors, the design of the shower scene also serves to increase the tension of the drama. The scene's staccato editing with its barrage of extreme angles makes the audience feel attacked along with Marion Crane. Like Marion, the viewer does not know when or where the next stab is coming from, or even who is behind the attack. So vivid is the depiction that when some viewers recalled the scene after viewing it for the first time, they described it, incorrectly, as being in color.

Film historian Stephen Rebello summed up the shower scene this way: "Hitchcock simultaneously succeeded in titillating and shocking the viewer while concealing the nudity of the victim and the true identity of the attacker. Most crucially, the impressionistic montage so stylized and abstracted the action that the sequence was to devastate rather than nauseate the audience."[5]

CREATING TENSION THROUGH TEMPO

What makes the shower scene so powerful? Certainly the camera angles and Bernard Herrmann's masterful music score contribute greatly to the scene. The key to the scene's success, however, lies in its editing.

Over the years, many inaccuracies about the scene have surfaced, including how many cuts it actually contains. Many sources overestimate the number of cuts, with some claiming as many as ninety in a forty-five-second span. Although the number varies depending on when in the scene the count starts (when Marion first enters the bathroom to take a shower or when Norman enters), and when it stops (after Norman flees the bathroom or after Marion falls out of the shower-tub, dead), the greatest number is fifty-five in approximately three-and-a-half minutes. Regardless of the total number of cuts, the effectiveness of the scene depends in large part on the tempo of the editing.

Editorially the scene can be divided into three groups: pre-attack, attack, and post-attack. The first eleven shots of the pre-attack begin with Marion flushing torn pieces of an incriminating note down the toilet, disrobing, turning on the shower, and stepping into the tub. With the water flowing, she unwraps a bar of soap, then immerses herself in the flow and begins to wash, closing her eyes against the streaming water.

According to an interview with Janet Leigh, Hitchcock's goal in this opening segment was to suggest that Marion, having decided to return to Phoenix and confess, is cleansing her conscience as well as her body. "The shower was a baptism," she said, "a taking away of the torment from her mind. . . . He [Hitchcock] wanted the audience to feel her peacefulness, her kind of rebirth, so that the moment of intrusion is even more shocking and tragic."[6]

Appropriately the pace of the cuts in this section is even and moderate. Along with the sound of the running water, the steadiness of the editing, from one medium shot to the next, is soothing. Many of the shots include slow camera pans that also contribute to a feeling of calm.

In the twelfth shot, Marion, still engrossed in her cleaning, stands in the right foreground facing the camera, an opaque shower curtain behind her. As the camera slowly pushes in, the bathroom door opens and the shadowy figure of Norman, dressed in his "Mother" garb, enters. (According to various sources, a tall stunt woman actually portrayed Norman in this scene, not Anthony Perkins. Hitchcock kept her face obscured through lighting and black face paint.) After a dramatic pause, Norman flings open the curtain and raises a huge

knife over his head. At the same moment, high-pitched string music, like screeching birds, fills the soundtrack.

This sixteen-second shot is followed by a series of very quick shots depicting Norman's brutal stabbing of Marion. Norman plunges his knife repeatedly into Marion, and with every stab, a new angle of her body is seen—a tight close-up of her

Hitchcock uses a butter knife to re-enact his famous scene from **Psycho.**

screaming mouth, a medium shot of her lower legs, watery blood swirling around them, overhead shots of her torso as she tries to protect her chest from Norman's knife, etc.

Thirty-three distinct shots unfold in approximately twenty-three seconds. Although the pace of the shots is fast throughout the attack section, the tempo increases even more during the final volley of stabs. The force of the editing mirrors the force of the attack, heightening the subjective feel of the scene.

Then, just as suddenly as it began, the attack ends. As Norman sprints from the bathroom and Marion takes her last gasps, the tempo of the editing slows instantly. Accompanied by thudding, low-pitched orchestral chords, the first shot after Norman's exit is a close-up of Marion's hand twitching against the shower wall. Following this six-second shot is an eighteen-second shot of a glassy-eyed Marion sliding down the shower wall. Coming after the fast-paced attack shots, these two shots feel especially protracted and dramatic.

In another six-second close-up of her hand, Marion grasps the shower curtain and pulls on it with her dying breath. A series of three quick shots, including a shot looking directly up at the gushing showerhead, shows the curtain tearing from its rings and Marion falling forward over the edge of the tub, her face hitting the floor. The music stops altogether, replaced by sounds of the shower's running water.

In another eighteen-second shot, the camera starts on a medium-close shot of Marion's feet, now lying sideways in the tub, follows a stream of bloody water to the drain, and ends on an extreme close-up of the drain. The circle of the drain then dissolves into an extreme close-up of Marion's eye.

In the most distinctive shot of the entire movie, the camera rotates around her eye and very slowly pulls back to reveal her lifeless face. (The shot reportedly was achieved with the help of an optical printer, which made the close-up a still image.) The "eye" shot lasts a full thirty seconds.

After a quick shot of the showerhead comes the last big shot of the scene. The camera returns to a close-up of Marion's face, then dollies slowly away from her body and travels out of the bathroom, pausing on a folded newspaper containing the stolen cash before stopping on a view of Norman's house from the room window. This final thirty-three-second shot ends with Norman in the far distance, screaming at "Mother" inside the house.

In some ways, the end of the scene cruelly mirrors the opening. Streaming water that was comforting in the beginning now is tinged with blood and seems to pound relentlessly. The gurgling of the water going down the drain is similar to the sound of the water and pieces of note going down the toilet. The draining water, however, echoes the draining of Marion's life from her body, not the purging of her guilty conscience.

In keeping with the montage concept, the overall rhythm of the scene—the rhythm of the camera moves combined with the rhythm of the music and editing—mimics the scene's action. The moderate tempo of the hopeful opening is followed by the increasingly frenzied pace of the attack, then the slowing tempo of the deadly end. Within each section, however, is some variation in tempo. The very long shots of the end, for instance, are punctuated by quick shots that help bump the viewer to the next point.

PUTTING IT ALL TOGETHER:

WALTER MURCH AND

APOCALYPSE NOW

Made several years after the end of the unpopular Vietnam War, *Apocalypse Now* struck a chord with audiences, especially younger viewers who identified with the film's antiwar politics and counterculture artistry. With its brutal depictions of battle, rock 'n' roll score, and stunning visuals, *Apocalypse Now* forever changed the war movie genre. For movie critic Roger Ebert, *Apocalypse Now* "is one of the great films of all time. It shames modern Hollywood's timidity. To watch it is to feel yourself lifted up to the heights where the cinema can take you, but so rarely does. The film is a mirror reflecting our feelings about the war in Vietnam, in all their complexity and sadness."[1]

Four picture editors, including supervising editor Richard Marks, were hired to compile Coppola's substantial amount of footage. Walter Murch, Coppola's business partner and frequent collaborator, was brought in last and edited the picture for a year, then worked on the soundtrack for another year. Murch is credited with editing every scene in the film through the *sampan* massacre, except the Playboy Bunny sequence, which was edited by Lisa Fruchtman. The complicated helicopter attack sequence was edited first by Jerry Greenberg, but was completed by Murch.

In *The Conversations*, Murch notes how the *Apocalypse Now* editorial team worked together:

> We were in and out of each other's rooms all the time, and there were screenings of the film about every month. . . . At a certain point . . . we began to have intuitions about how each of us was approaching the material. That's how it happens. You pick up the good things that the other editors are doing and you metabolize those approaches into what you're doing, and vice versa.[2]

In addition to his contribution as picture editor, Murch is credited with introducing sound design as a cinematic concept with this movie. Although not unheard of, Murch's close, early collaboration with Coppola on matters of sound was unusual in Hollywood. In their San Francisco facilities, Murch and a large postproduction sound crew conceived new methods for mixing and presenting the film's complex soundtrack. The movie was one of the first to be projected using quadrophonic surround sound.

The film's August 1979 opening was much antici-pated, and audiences were not disappointed. In particular, Murch's sound design and Vittorio Storaro's cinematography stood out. Roger Ebert recalled that when he first saw the picture in a theater, it "was so filled with light and sound that I felt enveloped; the helicopters in the famous village assault could first be heard behind me, and then passed overhead, and yes, there were people who involuntarily ducked."[3]

The movie earned eight Oscar nominations, including Best Picture and Best Editing, and won in the Best Cinematography and Best Sound category. In 2001, a "director's cut" version of the film was released in theaters. Titled *Apocalypse Now Redux*, the director's cut included forty-nine minutes of previously deleted material, remixed and edited by Murch. Although reaction to the added footage was mostly negative, critics and viewers alike agreed that the original still packed a considerable punch. Decades later, the film still reverberates.

WALTER MURCH

Of the many talented editors around today none is as influential and versatile as Walter Murch. The three-time Oscar winner is the only major editor who works on both sound and picture. His editing and groundbreaking sound design on *Apocalypse Now* helped make that picture the definitive movie about the Vietnam War.

Murch began his professional career in 1969, creating a "sound montage" for Francis Ford Coppola's film *The Rain People*. Sound was Murch's first obsession as an artist, having studied it as a boy growing up in New York. After *The Rain People*, Murch cowrote and did sound for *THX 1138* (1971), George Lucas's first feature film. Around the same time, Murch, Lucas, and Coppola teamed up to form American Zoetrope in northern California, the first significant movie studio in the region. Murch then worked as the supervising sound editor on Coppola's *The Godfather* (1972), and as a sound mixer on Lucas's *American Graffiti* (1973). Ironically, the first film on which Murch is credited as picture editor was *The Conversation*, Coppola's 1974 suspense mystery about a sound surveillance expert (Gene Hackman). Murch also worked with Coppola on *The Godfather, Part II* (1974) and *The Godfather, Part III* (1990).

Besides Coppola and Lucas, Murch has collaborated with many top-notch directors, including Philip Kaufman (*The Unbearable Lightness of Being*), Anthony Minghella (*The English Patient, Cold Mountain*), and Sam Mendes (*Jarhead*).

Gene Hackman in a scene from Francis Ford Coppola's 1974 film **The Conversation**

THE STORY

Apocalypse Now is based loosely on Joseph Conrad's 1902 novella *Heart of Darkness*. The novella chronicles English sailor Marlow's journey down an African river and his encounter with Kurtz, a once high-minded Belgian trader who has gone insane in the jungle wilds. For the movie, Coppola and co-screenwriter John Milius changed the Marlow character into an Army captain named

Benjamin L. Willard, and Africa into Southeast Asia during the Vietnam War. The story's antagonist is still a man named Kurtz, but instead of a trader, he is an Army colonel. Like the novel, the film attempts through its tone as well as its plot to portray a violent world out of balance.

Although burnt out from battle, Willard (Martin Sheen) receives orders in Saigon to lead a secret mission into the jungles of Cambodia, where Colonel Walter E. Kurtz (Marlon Brando), a Special Forces Green Beret, is hiding out. The highly decorated Kurtz has apparently suffered a mental breakdown and is killing indiscriminately. Anxious to shut down Kurtz and his illegal operation, military officials instruct Willard, a former special operations officer, to find and assassinate the colonel.

To reach Kurtz, Willard must travel the Nung River on a river patrol boat, manned by a crew of three young sailors—Chef, Lance, and Clean—and a skipper, Chief. The journey proves deadly and disturbing, as military order has virtually disinte-grated in the horrors of the jungle. By the time the boat reaches the Cambodian village where Kurtz awaits him, Willard is exhausted and psychologically spent. In the end, however, Willard completes his mission, slaughtering the compliant Kurtz with a machete.

BREAKING IT DOWN

Although *Apocalypse Now* contains many memorable sequences, none are more compelling than its opening. As author Michael Ondaatje observed in his interview book *The Conversations*, the opening "seems to cradle all aspects and moments of the film, as well as introducing us to Willard."[4] Pulling some footage and sounds from other scenes, Murch created a riveting film-within-a-film. No sequence in the movie is more defined by its editing and soundtrack than the first one.

THE BEGINNING AND "THE END"

The first moments of the seven-and-a-half-minute opening begin in total darkness. Before the first image appears, the soft, distended sound of a helicopter's turning blades (described by Murch as *whooh whooh whooh*) are heard. The screen then fills with an extreme long shot of a stand of jungle palms. In slow motion a helicopter enters and crosses the frame from the left, and the yellow smoke of napalm swirls up in the foreground. This image continues until finally, a full minute into the film, the first notes of The Doors moody song "The End" begin to play on the soundtrack.

Still on the same shot, Jim Morrison sings the song's first line, "This is the end, my friend," and the trees explode in an immense fiery ball. The camera tracks right, revealing more trees going up in flames and more helicopters crossing back and

Helicopters, tanks, and exploding napalm dominate this scene from Apocalypse Now *(1979).*

forth. The only sounds heard are the helicopter blades and the music, no blasts or crackling fire.

The long shot continues for another thirty seconds, then an extreme close-up of Willard's upside-down face appears superimposed over the tracking jungle footage. Fire and helicopters are still visible in the bottom right of the frame but Willard's slightly sweaty face dominates. After about ten seconds, a third image of a turning ceiling fan appears on top of the other two. On the soundtrack, the song has grown louder and taken over from the helicopter blades. The ceiling fan disappears and is replaced by the face of a primitive stone statue, glimpsed on the far right of the screen.

Over the next minute or so, the visual emphasis of the multiple images shifts back and forth from fiery jungle with helicopters, to Willard's upside-down face, to the fan. At one point, the camera circles around Willard's face, adding to the visual confusion. Similarly, the soundtrack shifts from the song to the helicopter blades and back again.

Murch's montage works immediately on two levels. First, through the blending and blurring of images and sound, the montage establishes the film's narrative tone. The audience is brought into a setting that is very real and violent, but at the same time, beautifully dreamlike and hypnotic. Even the yellow napalm smoke appears enticing. This feeling extends throughout the movie and becomes part of the story itself. As he later moves up the river in his

***Martin Sheen as Captain Benjamin L. Willard in a key scene from** Apocalypse Now*

boat, Willard will find he is both repulsed by and drawn into the jungle and the war.

Mixing the images this way, especially using close-ups of Willard's thoughtful face, suggests that he is remembering a past experience. Through his editing, Murch immediately connects Willard to the burning jungle. Already the audience suspects that he is somehow involved in the destruction on the screen.

This notion is reinforced in the next series of superimposed shots, beginning with a slow, sweeping close-up of objects on a nightstand—dog tags, official documents, pages of a handwritten letter, foreign currency, and a photo of a young woman.

The shot continues to Willard, his head now clearly seen resting on a pillow, eyes closed, and reveals more objects surrounding him, most notably a glass half filled with whiskey and a whiskey bottle. Then the camera moves to reveal what is lying right next to Willard's head—a gun. At the same moment, Jim Morrison sings, "And all the children are insane."

All of this footage is superimposed over the burning jungle, visible in the corner of the frame. The juxtaposition of the song's lyrics and the image of the gun hints that Willard might be suicidal. On the next close-up of Willard's face, the song begins to fade away while the distorted sound of the helicopter blades gets louder and louder. The superimposed imaging stops.

The rest of the scene, beginning with a low-angle shot of the ceiling fan, its blades spinning in rhythm to the helicopter sounds, plays out in Willard's hotel room. Murch summed up the sequence to this point this way: "We're given fragments—jungle, explosion, upside-down head, Cambodian sculpture, flames, helicopter—disjointed things. Then the disjointed-ness begins to congeal into a world . . . giving us at least enough context to proceed with the story. . ."[5]

Gradually, as the camera moves toward the room's shuttered window, the distorted "dream" helicopter sounds are replaced by the sound of a real helicopter flying over Willard's hotel. Now up, Willard peeks through the shutters at the sun-drenched street below.

STILL IN SAIGON

At this point (a little more than four minutes into the film) voice-over narration, spoken by Sheen as Willard, begins. City sounds suddenly replace helicopter noises. As Willard takes in the busy street below, he laments that he is "still in Saigon." Over a series of shots, Willard then reveals in the narration his desire to "wake up back in the jungle again" and his confused feelings about his failed marriage and his continued participation in the war. "When I was here," he says, "I wanted to be there. When I was there, all I could think of was getting back to the jungle."

Though they all take place in the hotel room, the edits in this section are not continuous but are jump cuts. Through these visual jumps Murch suggests jumps in time—the long period that Willard spends alone in the room. He also conveys his sense of entrapment ("the walls closing in") and his yearning for his "next assignment." Murch underscores Willard's state of mind by adding soft jungle noises—crickets and birds—to the soundtrack.

In the final ninety seconds of the sequence, a half-naked Willard performs a drunken tai chi combat routine in his hotel room. The frantic, loud conclusion of "The End" takes over the soundtrack. The burning jungle images return, superimposed over jump cuts of Willard moving erratically around the room. Among the superimposed images are dark close-ups of Willard, his face painted with camouflage colors.

Recording Man and Insects

Written by famed Vietnam reporter Michael Herr, the voice-over of *Apocalypse Now* is one of the film's most memorable components. Although screenwriter John Milius included some narration in his original script, the voice-over went through many changes and was recorded late in the filmmaking process. Walter Murch oversaw the recording and was largely responsible for integrating it into the film.

In *The Conversations*, Murch states that inspiration for recording the narration came from a story he heard about John Huston's 1956 picture *Moby Dick*. According to Murch, Huston was dissatisfied with the stilted way that actor Richard Basehart was reading the lines of his "Ishmael" narration during a recording session, but when he whispered an aside into the microphone, his voice was relaxed and natural. Huston then instructed Basehart to whisper the entire narration.

To achieve a similar effect with Martin Sheen, Murch positioned the microphone "perfectly" and gave him the following instructions:

> I asked Marty to imagine that the microphone was somebody's head on the pillow next to him, and that he was just talking to her with that kind of intimacy. . . . In the final mix we took the single soundtrack of his voice and spread it across all three speakers behind the screen, so there's just a soft wall of this intimate sound enveloping the audience.[6]

For the sound of chirping crickets heard in the opening, Murch chose not to go out into a field and record a "thousand crickets," as he normally would do. Instead, he notes,

> We wanted a hallucinatory clarity. . . . We wanted something that was hyperreal. We got it by recording individual crickets very close, then electronically multiplying them till we had a thousand crickets. It's as if they each had their own little radio mike on. Then we had a thousand tracks of crickets.[7]

These shots of Willard's camouflage-painted face actually come from the film's end—just before Willard kills Kurtz—and function here as foreshadowing, or glimpses into the future.

Willard's out-of-control dance climaxes when he breaks a mirror with a punch and slices his hand on the broken glass. As the last chords of The Doors' song play out, Willard, oblivious to his injury, collapses on the floor, crying. In the next scene, army personnel show up at Willard's door, ready to escort him to his next assignment. Willard collects himself, never again to expose his inner demons in such a raw fashion.

According to Murch, Willard's behavior in the hotel scene was unscripted and acted spontaneously by Sheen. Murch took Sheen's intense, disturbing performance and, using his editing and sound expertise, turned it into a powerful thematic prologue for the rest of the movie.

CAREERS IN EDITING

"The editing process is tedious work—viewing hours of footage, then assembling a film a half-second at a time. I like to think this is sort of a cross between a short-order cook and a brain surgeon. Sometimes you're doing incredibly delicate things. Two frames different will mean whether the film is a success or not."[1] As Walter Murch observes, film editing requires a great deal of patience and sensitivity. While editors, like directors, enjoy making creative decisions, they prefer the quieter, less pressured environment of the editing room to the busy production set.

Unlike writing and directing, which tend to be all-or-nothing pursuits, editing offers a range of jobs that aspiring professionals can get started in. Many editors begin their editing careers working in commercials and music videos. Almost all picture editors begin as assistants and learn the finer points of cutting from veteran editors. Aspiring sound mixers and editors can gain experience through work in radio stations, with music groups, or in music videos, or by adding audio to Internet sites. Below, editors and assistant editors discuss their career path and offer insights and advice for those who wish to follow in their footsteps.

BILLY WEBER (EDITOR, TOP GUN, NACHO LIBRE)

The Oscar-nominated Weber, who worked his way up through the studio system, insists that being a computer whiz is not a requirement for becoming an editor. "They have to learn how to edit on computer but they don't really have to be good at computers to do that. It's just a couple of keys and a mouse and understanding what the icons mean."[2] Weber also believes that film school, while very helpful for some, is not necessary for all. "My main assistant right now came out of the L.A. public school system in East L.A. He was really interested in computers and movies. And he had this natural gift for computer knowledge and used it to get involved in visual arts. He did slide presentations for big dances and parties and experimental films. He just loved it. He's really talented and someday I think he'll be a big editor."[3] In addition to being detail oriented and precise, Weber feels that all aspiring editors should be, first and foremost, "good storytellers."

A potential career in film editing offers a wide range of jobs in which aspiring professionals can get started.

DEDE ALLEN (EDITOR, *BONNIE AND CLYDE*, *WONDER BOYS*)

Dede Allen, who is best known as the woman who cut *Bonnie and Clyde* and *Dog Day Afternoon*, left editing in the 1990s to work as a studio executive. She returned to editing in 2000 and, while in her seventies, learned to cut digitally.

> Well, I would give the same advice I gave in the old days, which is learn where the scene is. See plays as much as you can, good plays, because that's where you'll really find out about the three act form and learn about performance—even though it's very different on film. Anybody can learn the tools. Look, if I can learn the Avid, anybody can learn the tools. I didn't even type, you know. Storytelling, performance and good taste are the key to being a good editor. If you don't have the opportunity, if you're part of a culture where you can't get to the theater easily, make sure you try to.[4]

THELMA SCHOONMAKER (EDITOR, *RAGING BULL*, *THE DEPARTED*)

> Whenever I talk to students, I say, "Look at old films. It's all been done before. So learn, look." I understand that some film students don't want to do that. But Marty [Scorsese] does nothing but look at old films, and he's taught me so much about the history of film. Those old films are an inspiration. It's like a painter going to a museum to

be inspired. And then from that inspiration, you do your own thing.[5]

LEANDER SALES (ASSISTANT EDITOR, *MALCOLM X*, EDITOR, *GET ON THE BUS*)

[Sidney] Poitier wrote that the best place to learn how to make a film is in the editing room, because you learn what gets used and what doesn't get used in the storytelling process. . . . I thought, "Wow, that's just where I want to be," because when I really started thinking about editing and talking with people, it was clear that editors dealt with everything—cinematography, sound, actors' performances, all of that.[6]

ERIK C. ANDERSON (ASSISTANT EDITOR, *LAS VEGAS*, *EYES*)

In 1985 I began pursuing my dream by majoring in film at Los Angeles Valley College. I quickly noticed that most of the other students liked directing their own projects but didn't care much about cutting them. To me, editing the film was every bit as important as directing it, so I volunteered to cut everyone else's projects. I got my first job in the industry in 1987 as a sales representative at Christy's Editorial Film Supply in Burbank. I also continued to work on student projects and very low-budget films to gain

Thelma Schoonmaker holds her Oscar while meeting the press at the 77th Annual Academy Awards on February 27, 2005. Schoonmaker won the Oscar for "Best Achievement in Editing" for her work on The Aviator (2004).

experience as a film assistant. Then, my big break came when I was hired as the film conforming assistant on *Madonna: Truth or Dare*.[7]

CONTINUING EDUCATION

As the above comments show, there are many possible paths to becoming a film editor. While a college education is not a requirement of becoming an editor, filmmaking classes provide students with hands-on opportunities with professional-grade equipment and real actors. Along with the satisfaction of seeing their stories up on the screen, junior filmmakers receive valuable feedback from both their teachers and fellow students. Understanding and appreciating the whole of film art makes for a smarter, more confident editor. College filmmaking classes also enable students to forge valuable friendships and professional contacts. Many of the editors mentioned in this book got their first jobs through people they met in college.

According to recent *New York Times* articles, over six hundred colleges and universities in the United States offer programs in film studies or related subjects. Over one hundred of those offer degrees in film production, some with concentrations in editing. At the University of Southern California, all film students "write a script, use a camera, edit film, produce a project, light a set, build props, even buy—or cook—the food for craft services, in addition to learning about the history of film."[8]

Schools with filmmaking programs are located not only in California, but also across the United States and Canada. Below is a partial list of four-year colleges that offer degrees in film production:

- Auburn University, Auburn, Alabama
- Brigham Young University, Provo, Utah
- Chapman University, Orange, California
- Colorado Film School, Denver, Colorado (AGS, AAS, and BFA degrees)
- Columbia College, Chicago, Illinois (Concentration in Editing)
- Depaul University, Chicago, Illinois (Digital Cinema)
- Drexel University, Philadelphia, Pennsylvania
- Florida State University Film School, Tallahassee, Florida
- Loyola Marymount University, Los Angeles, California
- Middlebury College, Middlebury, Vermont
- New York University, Tisch School of the Arts, New York, New York
- North Carolina School of the Arts, Winston-Salem, North Carolina
- Nova Scotia College of Art and Design, Halifax, Nova Scotia, Canada
- Penn State, University Park, Pennsylvania
- Regent University, Virginia Beach, Virginia
- Ryerson University, Toronto, Ontario, Canada
- San Diego State University, San Diego, California
- San Francisco State University, San Francisco, California
- School of Visual Arts, New York, New York

- SUNY College at Purchase, Purchase, New York
- University of California, Berkeley, Berkeley, California
- University of California, Los Angeles (UCLA), Los Angeles, California
- University of Central Florida School of Film and Digital Media, Orlando, Florida
- University of Kansas, Lawrence, Kansas
- University of Michigan, Ann Arbor, Michigan
- University of North Texas, Denton, Texas
- University of Oklahoma, Norman, Oklahoma
- University of Southern California, Los Angeles, California
- University of Texas, Austin, Texas
- University of Wisconsin, Milwaukee, Wisconsin

The following community colleges offer two-year degrees in media and/or film production:

- Colorado Film School, Denver, Colorado (AGS, AAS, and BFA degrees)
- Los Angeles Community College, Los Angeles, California
- Los Angeles Valley College, Valley Glen, California
- Minneapolis Community and Technical College, Minneapolis, Minnesota
- Scottsdale Community College, Scottsdale, Arizona

High school graduates can also attend one-year (nondegree) film schools. The New York Film Academy, which has branches in New York City, Los

Editorial Salaries (Union)

Apprentice Salaries	Assistant Salaries	Editor Salaries
As low as $624 per week	As low as $1,000 per week	As low as $1,480 per week
As high as $1,110 per week	As high as $1,500 per week	As high as $2,500 per week

Angeles, and London, has a one-year diploma program in filmmaking. The academy also offers a special summer program for high school students.

Although editors rarely make as much money as top directors and stars on a given film, they tend to work more consistently than actors and directors. And unlike directors or screenwriters, people with editorial skills have a much easier time breaking in, as they can begin as apprentices and work their way up. Sound editors make somewhat less than picture editors but still earn a respectable wage. As with any filmmaking unit, salaries vary depending on the film's budget and whether the production company is a signatory of the editors' union. Nonunion, low-budget productions, which often rely on young talent, pay less than union shows.

CHAPTER NOTES

INTRODUCTION

1. Ralph Rosenblum and Robert Karen, *When the Shooting Stops . . . the Cutting Begins* (New York: Da Capo Press, 1979), p. 5.

CHAPTER 1. IN THE BEGINNING THERE WAS THE CUT

1. Michael Ondaatje, *The Conversations: Walter Murch and the Art of Editing Film* (New York: Alfred A. Knopf, 2004), p. 31.

2. Edward Dmytryk, *On Film Editing: An Introduction to the Art of Film Construction* (Boston: Focal Press, 1984), p. 4.

3. Ralph Rosenblum and Robert Karen, *When the Shooting Stops . . . the Cutting Begins* (New York: Da Capo Press, 1979), p. 1.

4. Sergei Eisenstein, *Battleship Potemkin*, translated from the Russian by Gillon R. Aitken (London: Lorrimer Publishing, 1968), p. 14.

CHAPTER 2. EDITING FUNDAMENTALS

1. Karel Reisz and Gavin Millar, *The Technique of Film Editing*, enlarged ed. (New York: Focal Press, Ltd., 1968), pp. 216–217.

2. Daniel Restuccio, "A Chat with Editor Thelma Schoonmaker: This Feature Film Editor Has Enjoyed 30 Years of Working With One of Hollywood's Most Respected Directors—Edit This!—Interview," April 2003, <http://www.findarticles.com/p/articles/mi_m0HNN/is_4_18/ai_100401228> (February 28, 2006).

3. Edward Dmytryk, *On Film Editing: An Introduction to the Art of Film Construction* (Boston: Focal Press, 1984), p. 25.

4. Ibid., p. 28.

5. Reisz and Millar, p. 216.

6. Richard D. Pepperman, *The Eye Is Quicker: Film Editing: Making a Good Film Better* (Studio City, Calif.: Michael Wiese Productions, 2004), p. 7.

7. Ibid., p. 8.

8. Ken Dancyger, *The Technique of Film and Video Editing: History, Theory, and Practice*, 3rd ed. (Boston: Focal Press, 2002), p. 354.

9. *What Directors and Others Say About Editors*, <http://www.editorsguild.com/newsletter/SpecialJun97/directors.html>.

10. Sidney Lumet, *Making Movies* (New York: Alfred A. Knopf, 1995), p. 161.

11. Reicz and Millar, p. 243.

12. Lumet, p. 161.

13. Kevin Lewis, "School Daze: Leander Sales Graduates from Cutting Room to Classroom," reprinted from *The Editors Guild Magazine*, vol. 26, no. 5, September/October 2005, <http://www.editorsguild.

com/v2/magazine/archives/0905/features_schooldaze. htm> (February 28, 2006).

14. K. J. Dougton, "A Cut Above: Editor Thelma Schoonmaker Celebrates in Seattle," n.d., <http:// www.moviemaker.com/hop/editorial.php?id=147> (February 28, 2006).

15. Michael Ondaatje, *The Conversations: Walter Murch and the Art of Editing Film* (New York: Alfred A. Knopf, 2004), pp. 72–73.

16. Personal interview with Billy Weber, November 6, 2005.

17. Ibid.

CHAPTER 3. IN THE EDITING ROOM

1. Keith Brachmann, "What Directors Look for When Choosing an Editor," reprinted from *The Editors Guild Magazine*, vol. 17, no. 2, March/April 1996, <http://www.editorsguild.com/newsletter/dirlookfor. html> (February 28, 2006).

2. Personal interview with Billy Weber, November 6, 2005.

3. Michael Ondaatje, *The Conversations: Walter Murch and the Art of Editing Film* (New York: Alfred A. Knopf, 2004), p. 43.

4. Edward Dmytryk, *On Film Editing: An Introduction to the Art of Film Construction* (Boston: Focal Press, 1984), p. 2.

5. "Integrated Post Workflow Is Key to Survival on *Lost*," n.d., <http://www.avid.com/profiles/060109_ lost_dsnitris.asp> (Feburary 28, 2006).

6. Debra Kaufman, "The E-Ring: A Roundtable of TV Editors Discuss the Realities of the New Fall Season," n.d., <http://www.editorsguild.com/v2/magazine/archives/1105/features_roundtable.htm> (February 28, 2006).

7. Ibid.

8. Betsy A. McClane, "The Editor as Teacher: Tina Hirsch Addresses the UFVA," n.d., <http://www.editorsguild.com/v2/magazine/archives/1105/news_teacher.htm> (September 28, 2006).

9. "Adapting to Digital: Walter Murch," n.d., <http://www.apple.com/pro/film/murch/index4.html> (February 28, 2006).

10. Mia Goldman, "Dede on Digital: An Interview with Dede Allen," 2000, reprinted from *The Editors Guild Magazine*, vol. 21, no. 3, May/June 2000, <http://www.editorsguild.com/newsletter/MayJun00/dede.html> (February 28, 2006).

11. Damien Begley, "Andrew Mondshein: Editing with a Sixth Sense," 2000, reprinted from *The Editors Guild Magazine*, vol. 21, no. 2, March/April 2000, <http://www.editorsguild.com/newsletter/MarApr00/mondshein.html> (February 28, 2006).

Chapter 4. Sound Editing

1. "Ben Burtt Answers Questions About Sound Design of *Star Wars*," n.d., <http://www.filmsound.org/starwars/starwars-AQ.htm> (February 28, 2006).

2. Ken Dancyger, *The Technique of Film and Video Editing: History, Theory, and Practice*, 3rd ed. (Boston: Focal Press, 2002), p. 372.

3. Randy Thom, "Designing a Movie for Sound," 1999, <http://www.filmsound.org/articles/designing_for_sound.htm> (February 28, 2006).

CHAPTER 5. PUTTING IT ALL TOGETHER: GEORGE TOMASINI AND *PSYCHO*

1. Rachel Igel, "I'll Let the Film Pile Up for You, An Interview with Mary Tomasini," 2000, <http://www.editorsguild.com/newsletter/Directory/tomasini.html> (February 28, 2006).

2. Ibid.

3. *Psycho*, Collector's Edition (MCA Home Video, 1998).

4. Stephen Rebello, *Alfred Hitchcock and the Making of Psycho* (New York: St. Martin's Griffin, 1990), pp. 104–105.

5. Ibid., p. 117.

6. Ibid., p. 109.

CHAPTER 6. PUTTING IT ALL TOGETHER: WALTER MURCH AND *APOCALYPSE NOW*

1. Roger Ebert, *"Apocalypse Now/Redux,"* *Chicago Sun-Times*, August 10, 2001, <http://rogerebert.suntimes.com/apps/pbcs.dll/article?AID=/20010810/REVIEWS/108100302/1023> (February 28, 2006).

2. Michael Ondaatje, *The Conversations: Walter Murch and the Art of Editing Film* (New York: Alfred A. Knopf, 2004), pp. 61–62.

3. Ebert.

4. Ondaatje, p. 60.

5. Ibid., p. 261.

6. Ibid., pp. 64–65.

7. Ibid., p. 243.

CHAPTER 7. CAREERS IN EDITING

1. Michele Norris, "Behind the Scenes with Film Editor Walter Murch," transcription, *All Things Considered*, November 8, 2005, <http://www.npr.org/templates/story/story.php?storyId=4994411> (January 31, 2006).

2. Personal interview with Billy Weber, November 6, 2005.

3. Ibid.

4. Mia Goldman, "Dede on Digital: An Interview with Dede Allen," 2000, reprinted from *The Editors Guild Magazine*, vol. 21, no. 3, May/June 2000, <http://www.editorsguild.com/newsletter/MayJun00/dede.html> (February 28, 2006).

5. Norman Hollyn, "The View from the Cutting Room Ceiling: Thelma Schoonmaker and Martin Scorsese on *The Gangs of New York*," 2003, reprinted from *The Editors Guild Magazine*, vol. 24, no. 1, January/February 2003, <http://www.editorsguild.com/newsletter/JanFeb03/norm_gangs_of_ny.html> (February 28, 2006).

6. Kevin Lewis, "School Daze: Leander Sales Graduates from Cutting Room to Classroom," reprinted from *The Editors Guild Magazine*, vol. 26, no. 5, September/October 2005, <http://www.editorsguild. com/v2/magazine/archives/0905/features_schooldaze. htm> (February 28, 2006).

7. "Getting to Know You: Introducing Ordinary Members of the Guild, Erik C. Anderson," 1999, reprinted from *The Motion Picture Editors Guild Newsletter*, vol. 20, no. 2, March/April 1999, <http:// www.editorsguild.com/newsletter/marapr99/know_ anderson.html> (February 28, 2006).

8. Sharon Waxman, "At U.S.C., a Practical Emphasis in Film," January 31, 2006, <http:// www.nytimes.com/2006/01/31/movies/31film.html?ex= 1141275600&en=05f717679ebf1444&ei=5070> (February 28, 2006).

GLOSSARY

ADR (automatic dialogue replacement)— The process of rerecording dialog that cannot be salvaged from production tracks. Also called looping.

ambient noises—Naturally occurring sounds associated with a particular location.

close-up—A detailed view of a person or object. A close-up of an actor usually includes only the head.

continuity—The illusion of a real or logical sequence of events across a series of film cuts.

coverage—Shots that depict all of the action of a scene.

cross-cutting—The alternating of shots from two sequences, usually in different locations, to suggest the action is going on at the same time.

cutaway—A shot, usually a close-up, that is used to break up an action sequence. Frequently used to cover a break in continuity or coverage. A cutaway does not focus on details of the shot before or after it but cuts away from the action.

dailies—The first print made by the laboratory from an exposed negative, viewed daily during production. Also called rushes.

dissolve—The slow fading out of one shot and the gradual fading in of the next, with the two shots overlapping halfway.

dubbing—The replacement of dialogue after the visuals have been photographed.

editing—The continuous process of joining or splicing together one shot with others.

establishing shot—A shot that gives the viewer an overview of a scene setting, usually coming at the beginning of a scene.

fade-in/out—The gradual fading of an image from normal brightness to black screen (fade-out); or the gradual brightening of an image from black screen to normal brightness (fade-in).

fine cut—The final stage of editing a film.

flashback—A scene from the past that interrupts the ongoing action.

foley—The recording of custom sound effects. The term comes from the name of its inventor, Jack Foley.

insert shot—A close-up of some detail in the scene.

jump cut—Two similar shots cut together with a jump in continuity, camera position, or time.

juxtapose—To place side by side.

long shot—A shot in which a large area is depicted, often the entire setting of a scene.

master shot—A single continuous shot that contains the action of an entire scene.

medium shot—A relatively close shot, revealing a moderate amount of detail.

montage—Film editing, particularly editing in which images are connected thematically.

non-original music—Any music used in a film not written specifically for the film.

non-synchronized sound—Sound that is detached from its source in the film.

outtake—A take that is removed from the shot footage.

over-the-shoulder shot—A medium shot in which one actor is photographed head-on from over the shoulder of another actor.

parallel action—Two or more actions that take place at the same time in different spaces.

point of view—That aspect of storytelling dealing with who is telling the story and how it is told.

point-of-view shot (POV)—A shot approximating the view of a specific character.

postproduction—The phase of film production that occurs after principal photography has been completed.

principal photography—The main photography of a film and the period during which it takes place.

reverse angle shot—A shot in which the camera is placed opposite to its previous position.

rough cut—The crudely edited total footage of a film.

scene—A unit of film composed of a number of shots connected by a common setting.

script supervisor—A person who tracks which parts of a scene have been filmed and takes notes on continuity.

shot—Those images that are filmed continuously from the time the camera starts to the time it stops.

sound designer—The person responsible for the creative sound strategy of a production.

sound effects—Artificial or enhanced sounds, including natural and mechanical noises such as explosions, revving engines, animal cries, rain, and sighs, that are added to a film's soundtrack.

sound-on-disc—Sound recorded separately on a phonograph record and synchronized later with the filmed images.

sound-on-film—Recorded sound that is converted into a signal that can be photographed along with the film in the camera.

sound library—A prerecorded collection of frequently used sounds, such as birds and traffic.

sound recordist, or mixer—Audio engineer responsible for the recording and mixing of sound during production.

soundtrack—The audio portion of a film.

storyboard—A sketch or series of sketches that depicts how part or all of a scene is to be staged.

subjective point of view—Storytelling that emphasizes the perspective of one character.

synchronized sound—Image and sound are recorded at the same time.

take—One version of a planned shot, as recorded during production.

thematic editing—Editing in which images are cut together based on their dramatic meaning.

two-shot—A medium shot featuring two actors.

FURTHER READING

Chandler, Gael. *Cut by Cut: Editing Your Film or Video*. Los Angeles: Michael Wiese Productions, 2004.

Dancyger, Ken. *The Technique of Film and Video Editing: History, Theory, and Practice*, 3rd ed. Boston: Focal Press, 2002.

LoBrutto, Vincent. *Selected Takes: Film Editors on Editing*. New York: Praeger, 1991.

Murch, Walter. *In the Blink of an Eye*, 2nd ed. Los Angeles: Silman-James Press, 2001.

Ondaatje, Michael. *The Conversations: Walter Murch and the Art of Editing Film*. New York: Alfred A. Knopf, 2002.

Pepperman, Richard D. *The Eye Is Quicker: Film Editing: Making a Good Film Better*. Studio City, Calif.: Michael Wiese Productions, 2004.

Reisz, Karel and Gavin Millar. *The Technique of Film Editing*, 2nd ed. Boston: Focal Press, 1995.

INTERNET ADDRESSES

Motion Picture Editors Guild
http://www.editorsguild.com

Academy of Motion Picture Arts and Sciences
http://www.oscars.org

Cinema—Editing
http://www.learner.org/exhibits/cinema/editing.html

INDEX